MIXED BLESSING: THE ROLE OF THE TEXAS RANGERS IN THE MEXICAN WAR, 1846-1848

by

IAN B. LYLES, MAJ, USA
Fort Leavenworth, Kansas

U.S. Army Command and General Staff College
2003

Table of Contents

Abstract	1
Acknowledgements	3
Chapter 1	4
Chapter 2	14
Chapter 3	24
Map	26
Chapter 4	31
Chapter 5	41
Chapter 6	61
Chapter 7	72
Chapter 8	93
Footnotes	105
Bibliography	114

ABSTRACT

MIXED BLESSING: THE ROLE OF THE TEXAS RANGERS IN THE MEXICAN WAR, 1846-1848, by MAJ Ian B. Lyles.

The Texas Rangers assumed many roles during the Mexican War (1846-1848), fighting in both the northern and central theaters. Along with frontier knowledge and combat experience, they also brought prejudices and they earned a reputation for ill discipline. Thus, the central research question is whether the Texas Rangers contributed to the success of conventional army forces or did they materially hinder Generals Taylor and Scott more than they helped? Analysis begins by discussing the Mexican War, the Texas Rangers, and the concept of Compound Warfare (CW) (conventional and unconventional forces employed simultaneously to gain a synergistic advantage). CW theory is used to evaluate the Rangers' contributions. Ranger actions in support of Taylor's first battles and his movement to and conquest of Monterey, followed by the Battle of Buena Vista are described and evaluated. The Rangers' counter-guerilla operations in both theaters are evaluated next. The conclusion is that the Texas Rangers did contribute positively overall to the success of American commanders throughout the war despite some problems and atrocities. The final chapter also discusses the work's current relevance and suggests way for today's commanders to avoid problems when integrating irregular forces from differing cultures into the laws of war.

The opinions and conclusions expressed herein are those of the author and do not necessarily represent the views of the U.S. Army Command and General Staff College or any other governmental agency.

ACKNOWLEDGEMENTS

To Colonel Clay Edwards, thank you for the inspiration for this project and for your patience and guidance throughout the process of researching and writing the story of the Mexican War Texas Rangers. Thanks also to my brother, Ward Ferguson, for helping me refine my ideas and articulate them on paper. Every reader of this work should join me in grateful appreciation of his proofreading efforts. I would also like to recognize the love and support of my parents who taught me an appreciation of Texas history from an early age; I have you to thank for my success. Finally, to the memory of the Texas Rangers of old, they may not have always been right, but they were never deterred. It is to them, and men like them, to whom we owe our freedom.

Then mount and away! give fleet steed the rein
The Ranger's at home on the prairies again;
Spur! Spur in the chase, dash on to the fight,
Cry vengeance for Texas! and God speed the right.

Texas Rangers song

CHAPTER 1 - INTRODUCTION

On 22 December 1845, the United States of America annexed the Republic of Texas.[1] By May of 1846, the United States was at war with Mexico. When the sound of the bugle and the smoke of the musket faded from the battlefield, American troops held Mexico City and had "conquered a peace" that ceded nearly one half of Mexico's national territory to the United States.[2] While the war between the United States and Mexico lasted just two years, from 1846 to 1848, the circumstances that led to the United States' first foreign conflict began much earlier. The consequences of this conflict have lasted far longer than the fighting, and continue to affect U.S.-Mexican relations.[3]

Although much regarding this war is well known, at least to military historians, many aspects of these campaigns remain clouded by time. This manuscript endeavors to rescue one facet of this war from historical obscurity: the tactical and operational contributions of the Texas Rangers. Were the Texas Rangers effective in wartime? Did this irregular force of cavalry facilitate American success on the field of battle, or did the Rangers impede Regular Army units in combat? How did Generals Zachary Taylor and Winfield Scott integrate the Texas Rangers into their respective armies and campaign plans? Did they lack discipline and if so, did their lack of discipline create more problems than it solved? Did the Texas Rangers, as irregular cavalry, contribute measurably to the success of conventional army forces or did they hinder Generals Taylor and Scott during the Mexican War?

The U. S. Army's execution of the war consisted of three campaigns, two major (under Zachary Taylor and Winfield Scott) and one minor (under Steven Watts

Kearny). Taylor attacked west from Texas to Monterey and Buena Vista. Scott landed his army at Vera Cruz and culminated in the capture of Mexico City and the Treaty of Guadalupe Hidalgo. Kearny's campaign into New Mexico and California will not be discussed, as the Texas Rangers played no part in that endeavor.

In order to provide the reader a more complete understanding of this enigmatic organization, this analysis focuses on the Texas Rangers' influence at the operational and tactical levels while serving as irregular cavalry, scouts, and dismounted infantry during the Mexican War. Who were these mounted men from Texas and what prepared them to be able to accomplish the tasks listed above with no additional training and minimal outside support?

The Texas Ranger's lineage grew out of the frontier military tradition; where frontiersmen banded together in time of danger under their own leaders to confront the threat then disbanded and returned to their homes once the threat had passed. Although similar, this was not a militia, no prior formalized organization or roster of names existed. Rather, men volunteered to face the crisis, of their own accord or later with the blessing and authority of the Republic of Texas, provided their own arms and horses and rode forth to seek out and punish the offending group, rather like the posse popularized in modern Westerns. Once formed, "companies" of varying strength "ranged" the map of Texas, pursuing marauding Comanche war parties, harrying retreating groups of Mexican invaders, and seeking to ambush Mexican bandits en route to the relative safety of the border. At other times, the companies lacked a specific enemy and instead ranged the frontier patrolling in search of bandits and Indians, thus giving rise to the term "Rangers." This represented a slow evolution between the earlier posses formed only in response to a specific crisis and later organizations that were more formalized in nature and closer to a standing volunteer militia.

Shared need and strong leadership held these early Ranger companies together, leadership proven under fire as many Ranger "Captains" recruited based on personal reputations for bravery and tactical prowess gained in previous battles. However, this loose organization style and come-and-go attitude caused problems during the Rangers integration into the Regular Army's organization for the Mexican War. The Rangers had much more previous mounted combat experience than any other unit in the war but also brought with them a distinct operational style that appears undisciplined in comparison to Regular Army rules and regulations.

The men who formed the Texas Ranger companies of the Mexican War learned to fight mounted on horseback from two of the most unforgiving foes of their times: the Comanche Indians and Mexican irregulars and bandits. Of the Comanches, Fredrick Wilkins writes,

> Comanches had raided into Texas since Spanish days, but they had attacked the original towns. Initially they tried to be on good terms with the Texans, even though they came to steal horses. The Texans did not understand this form of friendship. By the mid and late 1830s, the Comanches and the Texans had begun a war to the death. The Comanches were the finest horsemen of their time, and their small tribal units developed into a warrior society. They were relatively few in number, or they might have destroyed the Texas settlers. As it was, they managed to

prevent westward movement beyond a certain line for decades.[4]

The Texas settlements did survive, due in very large part to the tenacity of the individual settlers and their collective self defense efforts; the forming of ranging companies.

After winning independence in 1836, the young Republic continually faced the threat of war with her much larger, former ruler to the south. In 1842, Mexican army forces invaded Texas twice, once in March with a cavalry force of 500 to 700 men under Brigadier General Rafael Vásquez and again in September with a larger force of 1,000 infantry and 500 cavalry under Brigadier General Adrian Woll. Both invasions penetrated as far as San Antonio with Vásquez' forces occupying the city for several days. Both armies successfully returned to the safety of the border without engaging major Texan forces; only the Rangers could mobilize fast enough to meet the invaders and they were too small to inflict any real damage.

In response, the Texans raised an army and set off to conduct their own raid into Mexico. Questionable leadership and internal dissention over the goals of the operation beset the army from the beginning and the expedition ended in disaster. Colonel William S. Fisher's Texan army, depleted by desertions and the fragmentation of its commands, numbered only some three hundred of its original five hundred men as it approached the border along the Rio Grande. The Texans arrived opposite Mier on 24 December 1842 and rashly decided to attack the Mexican garrison of Brigadier General Antonio Canales the following day. This in spite of the report of Ben McCulloch that the Mexicans had been recently reinforced by some 1,500 men under the command of Brigadier General Pedro Ampudia who had recently marched from Matamoros. Thomas Cutrer notes,

> Although outnumbered almost ten to one, Fisher entered Mier on Christmas afternoon and fought the Mexicans for twenty four hours. According to Canales, the Texans killed 40 and wounded more than 60 of his men; but Fisher believed that he had inflicted 500 to 700 casualties on the enemy and other estimates represent Mexican losses as high as 1,000. The Texans sustained a loss of 16 killed and 17 severely wounded. With food, water, and ammunition exhausted, however, Fisher surrendered, and his men were marched toward Mexico City.[5]

The sad saga of the Mier Expedition's fate did not end there. The Texans made an escape attempt near the village of Salado, but only three men made it back to Texas. Mexican cavalry swiftly recaptured the rest. The escape attempt infuriated Santa Anna and he ordered all of the prisoners executed. The governor of Coahuila refused and instead ordered a compromise; every man would draw a bean by lot, the Mexicans shipped off those who drew white beans to Perote Prison for years of hard labor, those who drew black beans (every tenth man) the Mexicans executed by firing squad.[6] The years of the Republic of Texas made a lasting impact on the men who fought as Rangers in the Mexican War. As Walter Prescott Webb explains,

> From long experience with Mexico, the Texans had come to distrust every word and deed of the race. The affair at the Alamo had taught them to expect no mercy; the Massacre of Fannin's men in violation of all law had

taught them distrust of Mexican honor; the fate of the Mier prisoners in Perote prison had taught them never to surrender; and the victory of San Jacinto taught them contempt for Mexican valor.[7]

Several Texas Rangers figured prominently in the Mier expedition: Jack Hays detected problems early on and returned to San Antonio; Ben McCulloch and his brother wisely departed on the eve of battle; and Samuel Walker was imprisoned at Perote. All of these men returned to Mexico during the war and each made significant contributions.

As noted earlier, neither the Comanches nor Mexicans took prisoners (except for torture, slavery, mutilation, and death) so the Rangers learned to shun taking prisoners in battle. In most encounters, both enemy groups could field numerically larger forces so the Rangers learned audacity and the value of firepower. Both groups were capable of living off the land and traveled long distances to raid the frontier settlements of Texas, so the Rangers learned to be hardy and self sufficient. Most importantly though, neither the Comanches nor the Mexicans valued diplomacy nor had they any dispute to settle, both groups simply preyed on the settlements as a source of plunder. In part because of this (and due to the prejudices of the era), the Rangers viewed both groups as barbarians and learned to seek no compromise with their enemies, the Rangers sought only to force their enemies to withdraw from the region and to punish them by killing as many as they could in the process. Wilkins goes on to add,

> The Texans had been receiving instruction in horsemanship from skilled instructors in a very harsh academy. By now they had

developed their own brand of riding based on what the Comanches and raiding Mexicans had shown them. These two were among the best in the world; if you failed an examination in their school it usually cost you your life.[8]

All of these skills and traits influenced the Ranger's conduct during the Mexican War; whether or not Generals Zachary Taylor and Winfield Scott learned to overcome these problems and utilize the Rangers to their full potential is a primary purpose of this analysis. Rangers fought in three distinct phases of the Mexican War: from Taylor's first battles through the fall of Monterrey, from Monterrey through the battle of Buena Vista, and along the Scott's lines of communication from Vera Cruz to Mexico City. However, the Ranger units that fought in Mexico changed over time as enlistments ran out and commanders returned with their units to Texas. Samuel H. Walker's company scouted for Taylor before and during the fateful battles Palo Alto and Resaca de Palma. John C. Hay's First Texas Volunteer Regiment, including Walker's company, fought from Taylor's initial attack into Mexico through the fall of Monterrey. Yet, this organization ceased to exist after the men's six month enlistments expired and the unit returned to the Texas border to disband.[9] Many of the men quietly returned to their civilian occupations and considered their duty to the United States fulfilled.

Recognizing the value of a ranger force and his need for security and reconnaissance, General Taylor requested that Ben McCulloch recruit a new Ranger company and return for duty with his army if hostilities commenced again.[10] McCulloch, like other Rangers, appreciated that the war was far from over and volunteered again to serve in Mexico. McCulloch's company fought with Taylor's forces as they advanced from Monterrey and gathered crucial intelligence on the strength of the Mexican Army prior to the battle of Buena Vista. General Winfield Scott also requested the services of the Texas Rangers. In response, Hays and Walker organized yet another Texas Ranger unit and conducted numerous counter-guerilla operations in central Mexico. The organization of this paper follows the timeline of the war and will evaluate the contributions of the Texas Rangers during each of the three distinct phases of the conflict involving the different Ranger forces as mentioned above.

Beyond the historical merit of this research, this analysis seeks to draw insights from the challenges of integrating, utilizing, and controlling partisan ranger forces. These issues confront the United States Army today and will likely continue to do so in the future. As the army prosecutes the Global War on Terrorism, the integration of regular standing army, or "main force," and "irregular" forces on the battlefield gains increasing relevance. Compound Warfare, a concept defined by the U. S. Army's Combat Studies Institute, illustrates the complimentary or compounding effects of main force and irregular units operating in conjunction on the battlefield. More succinctly, it is "the simultaneous use of a main and a guerilla force against an enemy."[11]

The rapid banishment of the Taliban regime in Afghanistan provides a modern day example of Compound Warfare, as American Special Forces "irregulars" directed and supported Northern Alliance main force fighters to accomplish this strategic objective. However, reports of mass killings committed by Northern Alliance fighters after the battle of Mazar-e-Sharif have tainted this otherwise stunning victory and highlight the risks inherent in this type of warfare. Similarly, the synergy achieved by combining main force regular and volunteer army units and irregular Texas Ranger cavalry on the battlefields of the Mexican War conferred many advantages to the American commanders and played a crucial role in many American victories. Yet, reports of atrocities committed by the Texas Rangers and their brutal reputation also caused serious concerns and contributed to the bitter legacy of that war. James McCaffery explains,

> No single group of volunteers was so universally condemned for its conduct toward civilians as were the Texans. One officer told how "they come here with the sores and recollections of wrong done, which have been festering in them for ten years, and under the guise of entering the United States service, they cloak a thirst to gratify personal revenge.[12]

No one has yet analyzed the case of the Texas Rangers during the Mexican War using the concept of Compound Warfare. The Texas Rangers fought alternately as guerilla cavalry, regular cavalry, and dismounted infantry during the Mexican War. Although their role as irregular cavalry most closely corresponds to the concept of Compound Warfare, it is probable that insights may be gleaned from analyzing the Rangers' other modes of employment during the war as well. What lessons can we draw from the experiences of Zachary Taylor and Winfield Scott as they struggled to effectively coordinate and control the actions of main and irregular forces on the battlefield?

Ranger history offers an example of Compound Warfare achieving victory against overwhelming odds. American forces fighting in Mexico always operated in difficult terrain, facing a numerically superior enemy, and among a hostile population who spoke a different language. The armies of Zachary Taylor and Winfield Scott also faced serious logistical challenges supplying forces over extended lines of communications that were constantly threatened, and sometimes interdicted, by enemy guerilla forces. The Texas Rangers' success at gathering intelligence and their unique ability to conduct counter-guerilla operations helped turn the odds in favor of American forces, but at what cost?

CHAPTER 2 - BACKGROUND

The Mexican War

The spark that triggered the United States' first foreign war, and only her second since winning independence, began in Texas. Spain's willingness to allow American settlers to immigrate to her northern Mexican territories set the stage for future turmoil and conflict. In 1820, Moses Austin founded a settlement between the Colorado and Trinity rivers in the Spanish province known as Texas.[1] The next year Mexico won her independence from Spain. By 1830, the trickle of settlers from the north had become a flood and Mexico, now realizing the danger of allowing large numbers of Americans to take up residency in a distant territory, issued a decree closing her borders to further immigration from the United States. However, Mexico had already sown the seeds of unrest by allowing the "Texians," as the inhabitants of the region called themselves at the time, many years of virtual independence and by doing little to foster allegiance to a weak and ever changing government in far away Mexico City. As Carol and Thomas Christensen note,

> In the first years after independence, Mexico encouraged settlement in its northern territories to promote national security and to protect its frontier from raids by the native peoples who had lived there for generations. Ironically, the Mexican strategy to safeguard Texas contributed to its loss.[2]

In 1835, when Mexico attempted to reestablish sovereignty over her unruly northern province, the Texians rebelled. A bitter war ensued in which

Mexico's harsh tactics on the battlefield earned her the lasting hatred of most Texians and many Americans. The massacres of the 187 defenders of the Alamo and of Colonel James W. Fannin's 342 rebel soldiers who surrendered at Goliad did much to fire the resolve of the Texas army and led to the crushing defeat of General Antonio Lopez de Santa Anna at San Jacinto, which secured Texas independence in 1836, or so the Texans thought at that time.[3]

If Texas provided the spark, Manifest Destiny provided the kindling. Manifest Destiny held that America not only had the right to expand to the continent's west coast, but that this expansion was somehow divinely ordained. The United States was obligated to spread freedom, progress, and American democracy across the continent, and those who toiled and suffered in ignorance or under the tyranny of lesser civilizations deserved to be incorporated into a better country. That the peoples of these other civilizations may not have desired this change mattered little. The United States was a young country, accustomed to rapid growth and looking for new territory to conquer. The idea of simply taking land was distasteful so Americans invented rationales to justify their actions. Manifest Destiny served this need well. Carol and Thomas Christensen note that "the term Manifest Destiny helped U.S. citizens to view their actions as both 'accidental and innocent;' it enabled them to rationalize and justify taking the territory they wanted."[4] Manifest Destiny was not new, instead it was a term used to describe an existing U.S. policy, that of westward expansion.

The bottom line was that America wanted more land and, in the opinion of many Americans, Mexico was not utilizing her sparsely inhabited northern territories properly, thus making them an inviting target for

America's expansion. Therefore, the choice came down to this: would Mexico give up land peaceably or would America seize it by force? By annexing Mexico's former province of Texas, the United States virtually ensured that Mexico would refuse to "sell" additional territory to the U. S. When diplomatic efforts failed, the Polk administration resorted to force; America would achieve her Manifest Destiny and it would be up to the U. S. Army to win it for her. The stage was set for war.

Onto the stage rode many memorable actors: Generals Zachary Taylor and Winfield Scott, Captain Robert E. Lee and Lieutenant Ulysses S. Grant. Santa Anna even returned for an encore. Zachary Taylor left the battlefields of northern Mexico to wage a different type of campaign. There too he was successful, winning the election as President of the United States in 1848. Winfield Scott won international praise and martial respect for his invasion and conquest of Mexico City, but the presidency eluded his grasp. Lee and Grant would meet again as opposing commanders during the Civil War and fight some of the costliest battles of American history. Santa Anna returned to the presidency of Mexico yet again only to see his armies defeated, his capitol conquered and his country humiliated. Many earned their place in history during the Mexican War, however few caused more controversy on either side than did the Texas Rangers.

The Texas Rangers

The Rangers began their official history shortly after the arrival of American settlers. From their inception, the Rangers would enjoy varying periods of official recognition and neglect, but always stood ready to defend their homes and settlements regardless of official sanction. Thomas W. Cutrer explains,

> The term ranger was first applied to Texas fighting men as early as 1823 when Stephen F. Austin commissioned ten officers to enforce the laws of the colony. For the next twenty years the force grew in size and responsibilities. Especially in the early years when the infant republic could not afford to maintain a regular army, the rangers provided an inexpensive and efficient frontier defense force. Most effective in small, well mounted squads, they were prepared to ride great distances at short notice to repel or destroy Indian raiding parties.[5]

The Ranger again enjoyed official status during the Texas war for independence. Formed by a decree from Sam Houston, Commander-in-Chief of Texan forces, and intended to safeguard the frontier from Indian raids during the war, the wording of the Rangers' inception ignited controversy. As Will Henry states,

> The Rangers were named a "special body of irregular troops." As such, they were entirely set apart from the regular army of Texas, as well as from her volunteer militia. This seemed like an innocent distinction at first, but it was not. It went deep into the heart of an uneasy frontier tradition of vigilante forces.[6]

For their part, the early Rangers seemed to care little for matters of semantics; they knew what had to be done and went about the task with a vengeance, sometimes in the paid employ of the Republic, sometimes not.

Although Ranger units fought in none of the battles for Texas independence, they earned a fierce reputation fighting Indians and Mexican bandits along the lawless frontier of the new republic. Charles Wilkins, a Kentuckian who traveled to Texas in early 1839 and rode with famed Ranger Colonel Jack Hays, describes the warfare along the Texas border,

> The reader must realize that he is to be taken to the extreme frontier of Texas, nearest to Mexico and the Indians, amid a mongrel population of Whites, Mexicans, and savages, living in a state of perpetual feuds, in which the knife and rifle are the sole arbitrators, in short, where all the stable elements and organization of society which afford protection in the decorous and staid proprieties of civilized life, are totally wanting. Strong men and unregulated passions exhibit their worst and best extremes in this atmosphere of license. History scarcely affords analogy to the fierceness of the Guerilla warfare raging among the three races.[7]

Some of Texas' citizens feared the Rangers would operate as a vigilante force under the guise of state control and to a certain degree these fears were realized; the Rangers operated on a modified version of the golden rule: do unto others (Mexican bandits, Indians raiders, and outlaws) before they do unto you. The Texas Rangers carried this doctrine of frontier justice with them into combat when they went to war in Mexico.

The nature of the Ranger's prior experiences in combat also caused them problems; their unique skills and attitudes made them at times both the most valuable unit in the army and the most controversial. The Rangers loose interpretation of orders and the rules of warfare caused consternation for their regular army commanders, as the subsequent analysis demonstrates.

The difficulties in controlling an irregular force that viewed virtually all Mexicans as the enemy is readily apparent, but the Texas Rangers also brought with them the benefits of an experienced light, irregular cavalry force with expert knowledge of the terrain of the southwest and unmatched firepower. Each Ranger carried one, or if he was lucky, two five shot (later six shot) Colt revolvers in addition to his rifle and Bowie knife. The cylinders of the pistols could be changed and each Ranger carried preloaded spares for his pistols. In this manner, the pistols could be rapidly recharged without having to meticulously pour powder, load each round, and affix a percussion cap. However, because the pistols had to be broken down into three parts to exchange a cylinder, it remained impossible to recharge while riding a horse under fire.[8] The Rangers also carried rifles instead of the muskets of the Mexican Lancers and the infantry of both armies. The rifle had much better range and accuracy than the smoothbore musket of the day and when used by the Rangers, either as a prelude to a charge or when dismounted and fighting as infantry, would prove highly lethal in battle against Mexican forces. Nevertheless, the Rangers now commanded a minimum of six shots per man, while some men carried considerably more.

Ranger tactics evolved over time into a highly effective doctrine of mounted combat. The Rangers initiated battle with well aimed rifle fire usually against the enemy leadership or the most effective fighters, delivered from outside arrow or *escopeta* (a Mexican muzzle loading shotgun similar to a blunderbuss) range. After attempting to kill or disable the enemy's leaders, the Rangers followed up with a charge to disperse the enemy formation; each man using his pistol or pistols at close range. The Rangers also learned to hold some forces in reserve (with loaded weapons) to cover the retreat of those that had run out of ammunition. If unable to break contact after expending their ammunition, the men used their bowie knives or swung the heavy Colt pistols by the barrels using them as clubs. This combination of audacity, fire discipline, target selection, firepower and shock effect proved a winning tactic on the frontier and served the Rangers well in combat in Mexico.

The Rangers also carried Bowie knives instead of cavalry sabers. This change probably reflected three causes. The first was the practicality of a carrying a field knife in lieu of a cumbersome saber that would be only marginally useful in camp. Second, the possibility of defense against the dreaded Mexican lasso; in close combat Mexican Lancers and Guerillas often lassoed their enemies and drug them to death behind their horses. The saber would have offered no capability (however remote) to cut oneself free from a lasso while being dragged. The final impediment to the use of sabers by the Rangers would likely have been the very practical reason for the absence of sabers in a frontier state such as Texas; its prohibitive cost.

Several "Texas Ranger" organizations fought in the War with Mexico. In fact, participants in the conflict likely referred to any mounted group of Texans as Rangers.

Therefore, the confusion surrounding these units warrants an explanation of the lineage of the various units that fought as Texas Rangers. First onto the scene came Samuel Walker's hastily organized company of twenty six recruited from in and around Corpus Christi and Point Isabel. They were sworn into federal service on 21 April 1846.[9] The actions of these men, and Walker's personal bravery, soon earned the respect of General Taylor and set a high standard for the Rangers who followed. However, this was not a cohesive unit and their collective inexperience soon caused them grief.

Next to arrive was veteran Ranger Captain Ben McCulloch and his experienced Gonzales Company. This was no ad hoc volunteer unit but rather a trained, experienced Ranger company on stand by for frontier duty. On 26 April 1846, General Zachary Taylor sent a call to the Governor of Texas requesting four regiments of volunteers, two mounted and two infantry. Colonel John C. "Jack" Hays, until recently the commander of the frontier battalion of Texas Rangers received the call and began recruiting the men of his former Ranger companies.[10] Thirty six hours after notification McCulloch's Gonzales Ranger company formed up and set out on the march to join Taylor, a testament to preparedness and an enviable timeline, even for modern forces.[11] This unit would make significant contributions throughout the course of the war.[12]

Upon annexation by the United States, the military forces of Republic of Texas underwent reorganization to bring them in line with U.S. militia laws. This process was incomplete by the start of the war, but the recently reorganized frontier militia companies would form the nucleus of Texan forces. Colonel Hays thus set about mobilizing the existing companies and recruiting additional men to fill the new authorization for a mounted regiment. The regiment was officially designated the First Texas Mounted Volunteers and consisted of approximately one thousand men under Hays' command. Samuel H. Walker served as the second in command with a rank of Lieutenant Colonel and Micheal L. Chevaille served as the third field grade officer with a rank of Major. Hays organized the regiment in June 1846 along the model of a volunteer regiment of cavalry as depicted below:[13]

1 Colonel
1 Major
1 Lieutenant Colonel
1 Adjutant (a lieutenant to be drawn from one of the companies)
1 Sergeant Major
1 Quartermaster Sergeant
2 Principal Musicians

The regiment was authorized ten companies organized as follows:
1 Captain
1 First Lieutenant
2 Second Lieutenants
4 Sergeants
4 Corporals
2 Musicians
80 Privates

Although authorized eighty privates, few companies enlisted at full strength. Muster rolls show Company G with seventy one privates, Company C with sixty seven, and Company F with sixty five. However, strengths varied widely with Company K listing only twenty nine privates, the average was fifty five.[14] The ten former ranging companies that comprised the First Texas Volunteers arrived with varying levels of experience on the western frontier and were sworn into federal service during June and July as they arrived to join Taylor's army along the Rio Grande.

The Second Texas Mounted Volunteers regiment organized under the same model with men recruited from the settlements of east Texas. The men elected State Senator George T. Woods to be their commander. Although lacking in frontier experience, these men also claimed the title "Texas Rangers" and shared the western men's aggressiveness, if not their experience. Combined, the two regiments formed the Texas division commanded by Governor J. Pickney Henderson who relinquished the duties of the state to the Lieutenant Governor and assumed the rank of Major General. The Texas division also included the First Texas Foot Rifles, but so few Texans deigned to serve dismounted that the unit was only able to form after a company of Mississippians agreed to reconstitute themselves as Texans. However, the Foot Rifles three month enlistments expired before leaving Texas and, unwilling to serve an additional enlistment, the men voted to go home, leaving the division with only the two mounted regiments.[15]

McCulloch and Hays both recruited and commanded additional Ranger units later in the war in response to calls by Generals Taylor and Scott. The composition, lineage and contributions of these units will be explained later and in the order they appear on the scene. Understanding the Ranger's lineage, organization and the background of the war, let us now turn to the manner in which Generals Taylor and Scott utilized the Texas Rangers in combat.

CHAPTER 3 - COMPOUND WARFARE

As mentioned previously, the concept of Compound Warfare (CW) provides a framework for analyzing the contributions and employment of the Texas Rangers during the Mexican War. However, to better understand Compound Warfare in its incarnation during the Mexican War it is first necessary to appreciate the purposes and motivations of the recent "allies" engaged in combat in Mexico under the flag of the United States. Dr Thomas M. Huber, the concept's intellectual father, notes that Compound Warfare can assume various forms.[1] CW is a complex concept and therefore deserves greater explanation. In the Mexican War, the relationship between the main force (the U.S. Army) and irregular force (the Texas Rangers) differed at the strategic and operational levels. In order to provide that explanation I will analyze each level in turn.

What was the relationship between Texas and the United States and their respective military forces at the strategic level? As mentioned above, Santa Anna surrendered to the Texas Army on the battlefield of San Jacinto in 1836 signing a treaty that recognized Texas' independence and established a border along the Rio Grande. In a remarkable act of good faith (considering the massacres of the Alamo and Goliad), the Texans released Santa Anna to carry news of the treaty to Mexico City. However, once out of danger from the Texans, Santa Anna reneged on the terms of the treaty and Mexico never recognized Texas as an independent nation. An undeclared war raged until the time of Texas' annexation into the United States in 1846. For the Texans, the war never ended; at the outbreak of hostilities, the *Telegraph and Texas*

Register wrote, "the war is renewed."[2] Rather than commencing a new war, the Texans just entered a new stage in which they enjoyed the advantage of a powerful new "ally," that of the United States.

The term "ally" highlights the fact that for ten years the Republic of Texas had warred with Republic of Mexico over its disputed southern boundary. With annexation to the United States in December 1845, Texas gained a powerful ally in its intermittent warfare with Mexico. A mere five months after annexation, full scale warfare erupted and Texas' new ally brought human, industrial and capital resources the former republic could never have hoped to match. In return for relinquishing its sovereignty, Texas gained the opportunity to permanently settle its border disputes with Mexico and settle some other old scores along the way, all under the flag of the United States of America. However, the Texans found their sovereignty difficult to part with, they clung to their independence even after recognizing the subordination of their military forces under the command of the United States. Sovereignty died hard in Texas; Texans voted to secede and join the Confederacy just sixteen year after entering the Union.

The United States needed no ally in its war with Mexico; instead, the concept of Manifest Destiny, detailed above, explains to a large degree the motivation of the U.S. government. President Polk sought to expand the territory of the United States, and Mexico was the obvious target. For the Texans, land was not an issue, it was the only commodity the Republic and later the State owned in any abundance, in fact they had more than they could control. For the United States western expansion served as a pressure valve for a growing population and territorial conquest as a path to greatness and international respect.

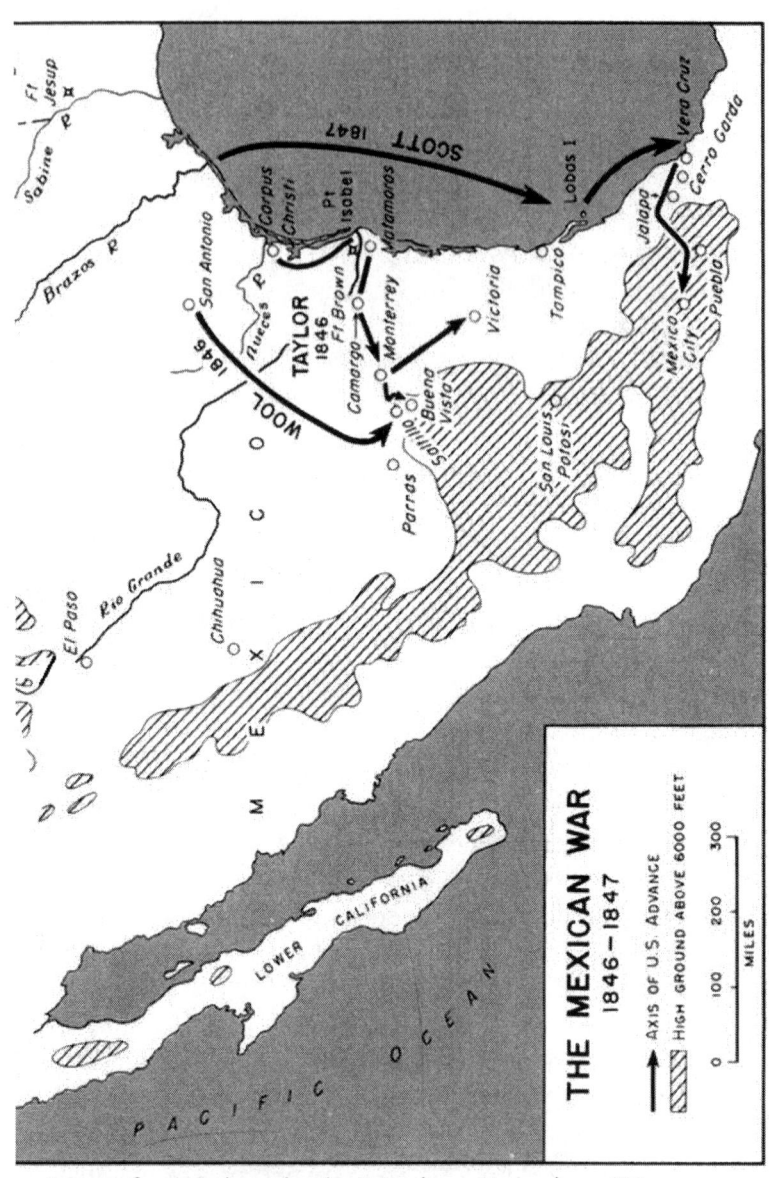

Map of operations in the Mexican-American War. From American Military History, by the United States Army Center of Military History, 1989.

The U.S. may not have needed Texas as an ally, but it wanted land and it would utilize the talents of the men of its newest state in the armed pursuit of its territorial ambitions. Texas provided land, men and perhaps more importantly, its border dispute with Mexico provided a pretext for armed conflict in which the United States could "conquer a peace" or, perhaps more aptly put, "conquer a piece," in this case a very large piece of Northern Mexico. If not allied in fact (and they were not, technically Texas was subordinated when annexed into the Union) the U.S. and Texas were united in purpose. If the Texans chose to think of themselves as "allies" so be it. This analysis, under the framework of CW, considers the United States and Texas as strategic allies fighting together against a common enemy much like the example described above in which U.S. and Northern Alliance forces fought together on the battlefield to achieve mutual strategic goals in 2001 and 2002.

Next we must discuss the relationship between the military forces of Texas and the United States at the operational level. At this level, the relationship differs from other levels. Generals Taylor and Scott each fought his own version of a CW campaign as a joint operation involving regular and irregular forces of the *same nationality*, not as a combined campaign involving forces of *different nationalities*. Operationally, therefore, this campaign more closely resembles George Washington's strategies during the American Revolution. Washington combined the effects of irregular forces (partisan units under commanders such as Francis Marion), which restricted the mobility of British forces and denied them information on Washington's movements, with the operations of his main force (the Continental Army), that arrived outside Yorktown to deliver the fatal blow, one the irregular forces were incapable of achieving.

The successful case of Compound Warfare in the American Revolution highlights many of the advantages inherent in this form of warfare. By adding a new star to the constellation of twenty seven, the United States improved its ability to "conquer a peace" in Mexico. Many of those from Texas who would volunteer to fight under the twenty eight star flag spoke at least some Spanish. Additionally, Frederick Wilkins, in analyzing the muster rolls of Texas units, calculates that some seven thousand Texans served in the Mexican War, a very high percentage from a population of one hundred fifty thousand or less.[3] Beyond sheer numbers, the Texans, the vast majority of which served as mounted Rangers, aided the conventional forces in several ways. As Dr. Huber notes,

> In many respects the operations of the main force and of the guerilla force are complimentary. The guerilla force provides important advantages to the main force. It conveys superior intelligence information while suppressing enemy intelligence, . . . [it] expedites their passage through enemy territory, . . . [and] interdicts [the enemy's] passage. The guerilla force may augment the personnel of the main force itself if need be, by adding to it combat power or labor at key moments. It may also attrit the personnel strength of the enemy. In sum, the guerilla force enhances the effort of the main force by offering information . . . and troops, and denying them to the enemy.[4]

The Texas Rangers provided some or all of these advantages to the armies of Taylor and Scott at different times during the course of the war.

By hitching their Lone Star to the constellation of the United States, the Texans also gained many advantages. For the Rangers, the most important among these was the safe haven afforded by the American armies, no longer would the lightly provisioned Rangers be forced to return all the way back to the settlements for safety and resupply. The Rangers greatly extended the range of their operations by departing and returning from forward American units. These same American units also provided them a secure base to rest and refit, funds for local purchases while scouting, and a source of resupply for weapons, ammunition, food, fodder and mounts.

For Texans as a whole, the United States Army offered the prospect of permanently ending the border war with Mexico. The American armies would do little to end the Comanche menace, but the Texans jumped at the chance to eliminate for all time at least one of their traditional foes. Gone were the days of the pinprick strike or the botched invasion. There was a chance to deal a death blow to Mexico's army. The Texas Rangers would turn all their considerable talent and hard won experience to steering and protecting Zachary Taylor's army until it could deliver just such a blow.

What of the motivation for men who marched to Mexico, fought, and died to settle the border and conquer new lands for the United States? Why did they fight? The Regular Army forces, never numerically large, fought because their generals ordered them to do so and they shouldered the burden of combat in most battles. The volunteer units joined for adventure and patriotism and fought for the honor of their states.

They carried the bulk of the fighting at Buena Vista and suffered by far the majority of casualties. The Texans, on the other hand, fought to redress past wrongs and to settle old scores; for them the war for Texas independence had never ceased. Still others joined to reap the spoils of war or to outrun justice for past misdeeds, these men did much to tarnish the reputation of the Texas Rangers and other volunteer units.

CHAPTER 4 - TAYLOR'S CAMPIAIGN: FROM PALO ALTO TO MONTEREY

The Opening Battles

General Zachary Taylor, encamped on the Texas coast, recognized that his force of regulars would be insufficient to win the approaching conflict and called for volunteers. Of the needs for manpower, none would have weighed on General Taylor's mind more than his dearth of cavalry; he could count on just four companies of the Second Dragoons [mounted infantrymen that also served as cavalry], none of them experienced with operating along the Texas frontier.[1] The citizens of Texas, long accustomed to war and rumor of war, quickly responded. Ranger Captain Samuel H. Walker arrived first on the scene and enlisted as a private in September 1845.[2] By April 1846 Walker had recruited a company and began patrolling Taylor's lines of communications and supply, gathering intelligence on enemy forces in the area, and carrying dispatches between Fort Texas, opposite Matamoros, and Taylor's main encampment on the coast at Point Isabel.[3]

In late April, Mexican cavalry under Brigadier General (*General de brigada*) Anastasio Torrejón surrounded and forced the surrender of two companies of dragoons, exacerbating Taylor's lack of cavalry and initiating formal hostilities.[4] Taylor quickly called on the Governor of Texas for four regiments of volunteers; two mounted and two on foot. As detailed earlier, the First and Second Texas Mounted Volunteers answered the call, but needed time to organize, equip and move to the border to join Taylor's army. In the interim, Captain Walker's small band continued to serve as Taylor's eyes and ears.

Mexican forces soon moved to cut Taylor's lines between his outpost across from Matamoros and his coastal base. During this period, Walker's men suffered an embarrassing defeat. Despite the frontier experience of some men, loose discipline and a lack of security led to a group of Rangers being surprised in their campsite by a Mexican patrol, resulting in five men killed and four being taken prisoner. This incident had the potential to dissuade General Taylor from relying on the Rangers, which as a Regular Army officer he was likely already inclined to do. However, two days later, Captain Walker, who had been absent from the camp when it was surprised, rendered a detailed report of Mexican activities to General Taylor and on multiple occasions crossed enemy lines carrying vital dispatches between Taylor's army and Fort Texas.[5]

At the battle of Palo Alto, Walker's company of Rangers served as regular cavalry and helped defeat an enemy cavalry attack.[6] Walker's men probed forward the day after the battle and helped determine the disposition of enemy forces at the Resaca de Palma. Walker escorted an artillery battery into position during the battle, but his company played little or no role in the subsequent infantry attack that unhinged the Mexican defenses.[7] However, General Taylor wrote in his official report of the battle that "I would mention the services of Captain Walker, of the Texas Rangers, who was in both affairs with his company, and who has performed very meritorious services as a spy and partisan."[8] Walker's bravery impressed the nation and restored Taylor's faith in the Rangers. In referring to this action, Walter Prescott Webb writes,

> Captain Walker, in the first engagement of the war, had set an example of heroic service for

all Texas Rangers to emulate, and had gained a reputation for the organization which every member felt constrained to uphold. This act of Walker's is significant of the character of the services rendered by the Texas Rangers in the Mexican War. Their acts often had a strategic value that was inestimable, upon which the fate of an army, a battle, or even a campaign depended.[9]

As for the "inestimable value" of the Ranger's contributions, the subject deserves more analysis.. However, it is clear that Walker's act renewed General Taylor's confidence in his irregular forces and secured for the Texas Rangers additional opportunities to prove their value.

During this phase, the Rangers caused few problems and provided a tactical benefit to Taylor's army by maintaining its ability to send and receive information from the outpost at Fort Texas even after Mexican forces interdicted the army's lines of communications. Walker's Rangers also identified the enemy's location and provided an estimate of his strength. This intelligence allowed Taylor to commit forces to reestablish his lines of communication, leading to the successful battles of Palo Alto and Resaca de Palma. The Rangers' activities and presence clearly aided General Taylor, and as he recognized the value of these unorthodox Texans he would continue to utilize their unique talents and capabilities in the future.

Invading Mexico

In these opening stages of the war, the Rangers served mainly as scouts and couriers, but they soon increased their value to the commander by conducting counter-guerilla operations and deep reconnaissance. After the Mexican Army withdrew in disarray General Taylor occupied the Mexican town of Matamoros and called on the Texans to reconnoiter possible invasion routes into Mexico in the direction of Monterey. Taylor also used the Rangers to secure his route of march by detailing them to serve as the advanced guard and flank security for his ponderous army. While the army gathered its strength at Matamoros, several additional companies of Rangers arrived and joined the American army, bringing the mounted regiments of the Texas division to nearly their full strength.

Ben McCulloch's veteran company of Gonzales Rangers departed from Matamoros on 12 June with orders from Taylor to conduct an extended scout for the army. Taylor listed the following as his intelligence requirements for the operation: to determine the location and condition of the Mexican army; to analyze the route in terms of trafficablility for the artillery; and to determine if the route was capable of providing subsistence for the army.[10] McCulloch also planned to engage in counter-guerilla operations en route. Although this dual mission likely seemed very efficient to McCulloch, had he known beforehand General Taylor might not have approved.

McCulloch's men scouted routes from Matamoros southwest towards Monterrey for ten days, but the Ranger commander delayed his return with the valuable intelligence for another three days while he conducted a search for Mexican Brigadier General Antonio Canales, infamous for his bloody cross border raids and a bitter enemy of the Texans. McCulloch accomplished the mission assigned him by Taylor, determining that the Linares route provided insufficient water to support the advance of the army and informing Taylor of the rumored presence of the retreating Mexican army at Monterrey. McCulloch's extended reconnaissance had the additional effect of clearing the immediate area of Mexican guerilla forces; they had fled to the northwest to avoid combat with the Rangers. However, McCulloch also demonstrated the willingness of irregular forces to act independently, seeking to achieve their own aims whether they were those of the regular commander or not. McCulloch's men rejoined the advanced guard of the army at Reynosa on 22 June.

Taylor next moved his main body north to join the advanced guard at Reynosa, then on to Camargo to stockpile supplies and gather his forces in preparation for attacking into Mexico along the route recommended by McCulloch. The general added the traditional cavalry missions of guard and screen to the growing list of tasks assigned to the Rangers. It was while stationed at Reynosa that the Rangers began to earn their reputation for ill discipline. The town was reputed to be the rendezvous point for numerous raids into Texas and many of the Rangers remembered mistreatment at the hands of the locals during the smoldering warfare of post-independence Texas. As one of the Rangers who fought in the Mexican War explains,

> Our orders were most strict not to molest any unarmed Mexicans, and if some of the most notorious of these villains were found shot, or hung up in the chaparral, during our visit to Reynosa, the government was charitably bound to suppose, that during some fit of remorse and desperation, tortured by conscience for the many evil deeds they had committed, they had recklessly laid violent hands upon their own lives! Quien sabe [who knows]?[12]

True to their frontier justice heritage, the Rangers utilized their own interpretation of the law, not that of the United States Army.

The Ranger's unruly behavior at Reynosa and Camargo underscored the difficulties of controlling an irregular force; these men volunteered to fight and, if left to their own devices, they caused problems. The Rangers held no monopoly on ill discipline or violence against the Mexican population. Other volunteer units also caused problems and committed crimes, but it was the Texas Rangers who held the dubious reputation as the worst offenders. However, the Mexican population, despite wrongs suffered, did not rise to resistance, and the army and Rangers moved on towards Monterrey.

The Rangers' actions during this phase obviously frustrated the commanding general, but they also greatly contributed to the success and forward progress of the army. Although McCulloch's counter-guerilla actions incurred some additional risk for the army by delaying the delivery of important intelligence, the benefits they accrued were proportional to the risks. Someone had to reconnoiter the route and if the Rangers had not conducted their counter-guerilla patrols, it is likely that Taylor's army would have suffered attrition and delay at the hands of the enemy irregulars. The Mexican population might have resisted but it did not. Did the Rangers' actions contribute to ill will against the invading army? Probably, yes. Would ill will have been present without the Rangers? Again, probably yes. If the Ranger's conduct among the Mexican population motivated some men to join the ranks of guerilla bands or take up arms against the invaders, it is not quantifiable how many and, regardless of the number, the impact was minimal. Despite the rumors of killings and the worsening reputation of the Rangers, Taylor not only kept them active in support of his army, he grew to rely on their unique services. Therefore, in the absence of additional measurable costs to the army, the activities of the Texas Rangers during this phase provided an overall positive benefit to Taylor's forces.

On to Monterey

McCulloch's Rangers arrived at Camargo on 9 July again in advance of the main army. From this base the Rangers conducted two extended scouting expeditions; the first up the Rio Grande to counter an Indian incursion and the second up the San Juan valley to further refine the Army's route of advance towards Monterey.[13] From Camargo Taylor's forces could advance on Monterey by one of two routes, upriver to Mier and inland via Cerralvo and Marin, or along the San Juan via China and Caderita. McCulloch decided to reconnoiter the China route first and he led his men southwest from Camargo on 3 August. He again had dual purposes in mind. As Walter Prescott Webb notes, "an incidental reason for choosing the China route first was because of a rumor that Colonel Juan N. Seguin was stationed at China with a band of irregulars, and McCulloch desired to capture him."[14]

Seguin, son of an old Mexican family in Texas, joined the Texans in revolt in 1835. In 1842 however, Seguin switched sides and joined Mexican General Woll in his invasion of Texas and occupation of San Antonio. The Texans never forgave Seguin's betrayal. McCulloch wrote Taylor from Camargo on 23 July imploring the General for permission to conduct another scout for the army and, if possible, to capture or kill Seguin.

> Seguin passed up the River San Juan a few days before we arrived here and might have

been overtaken. He had forty thieves and murderers from about San Antonio, to kill which would be doing God a service. It would be ridding the world of those that are not fit to live in it. They will never come to terms because they would be condemned by the Civil Laws and executed. Accordingly, they must do the frontier of Texas no little harm by robbing and stealing from its citizens. Any orders the General may give will be thankfully received and obeyed to the letter.[15]

Brigadier General William Jenkins Worth, one of Taylor's division commanders, soon ordered McCulloch's men to reconnoiter the routes to Monterey and granted permission to search for Seguin.[16]

The force departed Camargo on 3 August in the direction of China and Seguin. The Rangers narrowly missed an engagement with Seguin but did manage to capture four of his men. On the 6 August, they departed China to continue the scout. McCulloch rejoined Taylor's army on 9 August and rendered his report; the route towards China would not support the passage of the artillery due to deep ravines, narrow passages, and an impracticable crossing point of the San Juan above the village.[17] Taylor wrote, "this expedition has given valuable information touching one of the routes to Monterey. I shall dispatch another on the Mier route before determining which to follow in the march."[18]

Taylor again showed his reliance on the Texas Rangers. He again selected the Texans to conduct a crucial reconnaissance upon the results of which he would make decisions regarding the route of his army and the conduct of his campaign. Elements of

McCulloch's and Gillespie's companies departed on 12 August and returned five days later. Accompanying the Rangers on this scout were Captain Duncan of the artillery and Lieutenant Wood of the engineers, both along to determine the practicability of the route and to plan for the upcoming movement of the army.

On 19 August, just two days after the return of the Rangers, the Second Division under the command of General Worth departed Camargo beginning the army's movement to Cerralvo and on to Monterey. By 10 September, the army had inched its way forward to Cerralvo and poised to strike at Monterey. The Second Texas served as escorts during the movements and screened the northern flank. Hay's First Texas screened the left, or southern flank, conducting an extended scout from Matamoros to San Fernando through China and finally rejoining the army outside Monterey. Taylor's orders to Hays tasked him with "the communication of the policy of the Government, the ascertainment of the operations of the army of the enemy, as well as the feeling of the people, and the cutting off, capturing, or destroying [of] all armed parties."[19]

Taylor had previously detached McCulloch's and Gillespie's companies from the First Texas and established them under his command as "Spy Companies" even naming McCulloch his "Chief of Spies."[20] He now employed them as the advance guard of the army. Upon their reconsolidation, in mid September, Taylor looked to the Rangers to lead his army, for the first time in full division strength. On 17 September, Taylor issued his order for the final movement to Monterey, "the Texas mounted troops under Major General Henderson will form the advance of the army tomorrow."[21]

This phase shows Taylor's growing confidence in the Texas Rangers. Taylor detached the companies of Gillespie and McCulloch to serve as spies and scouts under his personal control and dispatched them to conduct reconnaissance expeditions in direct support of his army's movement. Taylor also employed the First and Second Texas in accordance with their distinct skills. He allowed the First Texas under Hays to operate independently ranging far to the southwest and into territory not previously visited by the invading American forces. The Second Texas he kept under closer reign, directing them to augment his Dragoons and serve as mounted escort for his advancing columns of infantry, artillery and supply.

The Rangers made several important contributions during this phase with few of the charges of ill discipline levied while encamped at Reynosa and Camargo. The Rangers not only successfully provided valuable intelligence to General Taylor, but their counter-guerilla actions, some officially authorized, some not, served to deny the enemy intelligence regarding Taylor's forces. The Rangers also expedited Taylor's movement to Monterey; his forces marched along the optimal route with little fear of being surprised by Mexican army forces. Taylor's movement to Monterey was uneventful due in large measure to the combined actions of his variously employed Texas Ranger units. Those forces undoubtedly rendered significant operational and tactical contributions during this phase.

CHAPTER 5 - TAYLOR'S CAMPAIGN: THE BATTLE OF MONTEREY

Isolating Monterey

On Saturday, 19 September 1846, the Texas Rangers arrived on the outskirts on Monterey in division strength, at the head of a grand army, and ready for a fight. James K. Holland wrote, "Texas went ahead today, now that danger is expected old Taylor has put us in front."[1] Soon the Mexican army would be paid in full for the Alamo, Goliad, the Mier prisoners, and ten years of border warfare, or so thought the Texans. Taylor also sought a decisive victory; he commanded some six thousand troops; 3,080 regulars and 3,150 volunteers including the Rangers.[2] He hoped to end the war in a single battle. In his path stood seven thousand regulars and three thousand irregulars under General Pedro Ampudia, and the defenders looked out from commanding fortifications and prepared positions. Clearly, this would be no bloodless victory.

Taylor's army encamped to the northeast, outside the range of the Mexican artillery, and began preparations for the assault on the city. Captain Gillespie's Company of Rangers, a company of dragoons, and a party of topographical engineers set out late that afternoon to conduct a reconnaissance of the city defenses, especially the western approaches. That evening Taylor finalized his plan; he would split his forces and attack from the west with one division while his main force of two divisions conducted diversions against the city's main defenses on the east. By attacking from the west Taylor planned to cut off the enemy's supply lines and route of communication to the interior of Mexico along the Saltillo road. Taylor also expected to fix the enemy's main body in the east while his First Division, under the command of William Jenkins Worth, conducted a turning movement to unhinge the city's defenses. This was not expert strategy. Instead the plan reflected Taylor's lack of heavy artillery with which to hammer the main defenses of the city.

On Sunday, 20 September, Worth's First Division departed Taylor's camp in the afternoon and, with Hay's regiment of Texas Rangers leading, set out for the western approaches to the city. No major actions other than various reconnaissances and preparations occurred on this day. The Rangers spent a cold, wet, and miserable night in a few mud huts and whatever shelter they could find. Hay's First Texas, including the companies of McCulloch and Gillespie, again led the advance on September 21. Nearing the Saltillo road, the Rangers encountered a mixed force of Mexican cavalry and infantry some 1,500 strong. While Hay's main body dismounted and assumed hasty positions behind a low fence, McCulloch's company charged the leading elements of the Mexican Lancers. The mounted Rangers discharged their pistols into the Mexican ranks as their dismounted comrades poured volleys of well aimed rifle fire into the enemy formations. As the charging Rangers crashed into the advancing Lancers, the heavy American horses slammed into the smaller Mexican horses and helped to check the enemy's attack.

In the ensuing close quarters battle, the Rangers' pistols and the rifle fire of their comrades proved more than a match for the Mexicans lances and escopetas. As the Mexicans began to retreat in disarray, American light artillery batteries unlimbered and began pouring shot into the fleeing formations. The retreat quickly became a rout. Several Rangers suffered lance wounds, but only a single Ranger died in the engagement.[3] The Mexicans suffered some one hundred dead and wounded including the Lancer's commander, Lieutenant Colonel Juan Najéra, in fight lasting only fifteen minutes.[4] Their attack broken and their leader dead, the Mexican survivors retreated towards the relative safety of the Bishop's Palace on Independence Hill.[5] Worth had cut the Saltillo road and isolated Monterey's garrison.

In this opening action of the battle of Monterey, the Rangers served as regular cavalry and executed a successful guard mission. By defeating Najéra's attacking Lancers, the Rangers prevented the defeat, or at a minimum the disruption, of the main body of Worth's division. Had Najéra's men been successful they might have inflicted serious casualties on Worth's forces and precluded them from isolating Monterey's western approaches. Even if less successful, the Lancer's attack could have delayed General Worth's attack to seize Federation Hill by several days. It did not. Due in large part to the success of the Rangers' guard mission and counterattack, General Worth was able to successfully execute his attack against Federation Hill in the afternoon of the same day; a significant operational and tactical contribution.

The Rangers subsequently maintained a cavalry screen west of Monterey throughout most of the following days of the battle thus protecting the American forces from a surprise attack by positioning themselves to provide early warning of approaching Mexican forces, itself an important tactical contribution.[6] No accounts of Ranger actions during this period mention any accusation of atrocities or other acts of ill discipline. General Worth remarked after the cavalry fight that he was "much pleased with the skill displayed by the Rangers in this engagement, and pronounced it a beautiful maneuver."[7] More important than the General's words were his actions, he next assigned the Rangers the task of joining the assault force and sent them forward to help seize the western approaches to the city.

Seizing the Western Approaches

Having secured their flanks and defeated the enemy's cavalry, both of Taylor's wings set about the task of capturing Monterey. In addition to the formidable defenses to the east, the city possessed two natural obstacles on the west: Independence Hill and Federation Hill. Federation Hill, the smaller of the two, stood four hundred feet high and to the south of the road into Monterey. Independence Hill was located to the north of the road and claimed a height of eight hundred feet. The Mexican defenders emplaced artillery on both prominences and fortified the existing structures. The Bishop's Palace or *Obispado* on Independence (a large stone building that was formerly the home of the local bishop) boasted two twelve pound and two six pound artillery pieces. Field fortifications covered the approaches to its rear (west) with a nine pound artillery piece. Fort Soldado on Federation possessed two nine pound artillery pieces with fortifications protecting its rear approaches.[8] Each hill mass was oblong in shape running from the northwest to the southeast and together they commanded the Saltillo road and the western approaches to the city.

On the afternoon of 21 September, General Worth made plans to attack Federation Hill. He selected a mixed force of four companies of red-leg infantry (artillerymen serving as infantry), under the command of Captain Charles F. Smith, and six companies of dismounted Texas Rangers, under the command of Major Mike Chevallie, to assault the peak.[10] The attackers, three hundred strong, moved out under the command of Captain C. F. Smith to meet the five hundred defenders on the heights.[11] Major Chevallie, never one to pass up a fight, deferred command to the Regular Army officer telling General Worth "There shall be no difficulty about that . . . I'll go under Capt. Smith."[12]

The assault force crossed the Santa Catarina River under ineffective Mexican artillery fire and paused briefly at the western base of the hill. General Worth, becoming concerned about the apparent Mexican reinforcements he had seen moving to engage the attacking party, ordered a second party (seven companies of the 7th Infantry) forward. As the first group of attackers began scaling the hill the 7th Infantry joined them and the two groups merged into one. Rangers and Regulars scrambled up the slopes stopping only to fire at the defenders. Upon reaching the crest of the hill, the attackers seized an abandoned enemy nine pounder and used against its former masters as they retreated down the spine of the hill toward Fort Soldado. Additional Mexican troops exited the city to join the fight so General Worth dispatched a third force; six companies of the 5th Infantry and Blanchard's company of Louisiana riflemen.[13]

As the Rangers and Regulars overwhelmed the defenses at the western end of the hill the third party began their ascent, a contest ensued as the attacking formations vied for the lead in the race to storm Fort Soldado. Captain Gillespie of the Rangers reached the defenses first followed closely behind by elements of the Fifth and Seventh Infantry.[14] The Mexicans retreated down the hill and into the city as the storming parties turned a second nine pounder against the

Bishop's Palace on nearby Independence Hill. The infantrymen set about securing their newly won fortifications as the Rangers descended the hill and returned to their mud huts to care for their horses.

Independence Hill remained in Mexican hands and General Worth ordered Colonel Hays of the Rangers and Lieutenant Colonel Thomas Childs of the Artillery Battalion to form a storming party and wrest it from enemy control.[15] At about 3:00 A.M., well before dawn on the morning of 22 September, three companies of the Artillery Battalion (serving as infantry), three companies of the Eight Infantry, and seven companies of Texas Rangers moved forward and began the assault up the steep slopes of the hill.[16] The attacking forces, numbering some five hundred men, split into two assault columns, Colonels Hays and Childs leading one composite group of Rangers and Regulars attacked from the south while Lieutenant Colonel Samuel H. Walker of the Rangers and Captain John R. Vinton of the Artillery Battalion led their mixed force in an attack from the north.[17] Both assault formations climbed during a storm that helped to mask the noise of their approach. Upon reaching the heights at the northern end of the hill the attackers quickly overwhelmed the Mexican defenders who fled down the spine of the hill and joined their comrades defending the Bishop's Palace. The Texans paid a heavy price for Independence Hill. Captain Robert A. Gillespie fell mortally wounded just after he led the final assault over the Mexican parapets. Even though he was shot in the stomach Gillespie still found strength to rally his men and lead by example reportedly telling his men, "Boys place me behind that ledge and rock . . . and give me my revolver, I will do some execution on them yet before I die."[18] The Rangers, having defeated the Mexican counterattack and exhausted from their early morning climb and the ensuing firefight, rested while their officers developed a plan to carry the last redoubt protecting the western side of Monterey.

The Bishop's Palace, with its heavy guns and stone walls, presented a dilemma to the attacking force; it might be carried by assault, but at a terrible cost in lives. Luckily for the attackers the guns of the fort could not fire to the rear. As the assault force engaged the defenders with long range rifle and musket fire and awaited new orders Lieutenant James Duncan's artillerymen disassembled a twelve pound howitzer and hoisted it up the hill in pieces. Rather than attacking the Bishop's Palace directly the American commanders set a trap; they would lure the defenders into a counterattack and ambush them outside the walls of the fort. A participant in the fight described the ambush,

> Captain Vinton came over, and I heard Colonel Hays advise him of a plan to try and draw the Mexicans out of the Palace, and it was at once approved of...Part of the force [Hays's] were to be concealed on the right of the ridge, and the balance [under Walker] were to take position on the left side . . . all to be hidden over the steep sides of the ridge . . . the Mexicans could be seen forming by battalions in front of the Palace.
>
> Captain Blanchard's company now advanced and fired. When the enemy advanced they [Blanchard's] retreated hastily back to our line, as had been arranged. The lancers rode boldly up the slope, followed by their infantry, eager to make an easy conquest. When they were close upon us, ... Vinton's men and Blanchard's company formed a line across the

ridge, and the two flanking parties [Hays's and Walker's] closed the gap completely across the ridge [behind the attacking enemy].[19]

The Mexican forces, facing massed infantry fire to their front and caught in a deadly crossfire from the heavily armed Rangers on each flank, withered and then broke. Some of the retreating Mexicans ran to the Bishop's Palace and slammed shut the heavy doors, Duncan's twelve pounder soon blew down the gates and the infantry and Rangers rushed in. A wild fight ensued, at times hand to hand, and finally an officer shouted "throw yourselves flat." The howitzer fired a double load of canister into the remaining Mexicans and the fight was over.[20] Only a few terrified Mexicans made it out of the Palace, they quickly fled down the hill and sought to rejoin their comrades inside the city.
Taylor's diversions against the Mexican fortifications on the eastern side of the city fared much worse than Worth's main attack in the west. Envisioned as limited attacks to draw the Mexican's attention away from Worth's actions in the west, Taylor's imprecise orders and his subordinate commanders aggression quickly led to costly assaults. On 21 September, Zachary Taylor issued the following order to Lieutenant Colonel John Garland now commanding the First Division, "Colonel, lead the head of your column off to the left, keeping well out of reach of the enemy's shot, and if you think you can take any of them little forts down there with the bayonet, you'd better do it."[21] These were not very clear orders for what Taylor intended to be merely a diversion, as events would soon show. The First Division's Regulars moved out on the left and General Butler's Third Division, manned by volunteer regiments, moved out on the right. The Second Dragoons and General Wood's

Second Texas received the mission to screen the right flank of the attacking force and if necessary to reinforce General Worth's actions in the west.[22]

A series of bloody attacks ensued, rather than a controlled diversion, and at several points in the battle Taylor found himself compelled to reinforce the attacking units. David Lavender notes,

> Having committed almost his entire 1st Division to this "diversion" Worth had requested, Taylor now had to bail it out. As Garland's men began to withdraw, Taylor sent Quitman's brigade ahead toward the tannery to steady them. It, too, took a terrible beating from the different forts and was ordered to fall back.[23]

Wood's Second Texas escaped the day's bloody fighting. The East Texas Rangers, screening to the north and standing by to support Worth, arrived too late to join the ill fated attacks on the east side of the city. Although Taylor's forces carried and held the *Teneria* (the tannery) and successfully diverted the attention of nearly the entire Mexican garrison the cost was shocking; 394 casualties, some ten percent of the attacking forces.[24] The eastern forces rested and regrouped on 22 September as General Worth's men seized Independence Hill at a cost of thirty two men killed and wounded during the previous two days of fighting.[25]

During this phase of the battle, the Texas Rangers served almost exclusively as dismounted infantry. This may seem curious at first, given the fact that the Rangers' fame rest on their exploits as a cavalry force, but the same characteristics that made them a formidable mounted force also served to make them effective when dismounted. Superior firepower, bold leadership and tenacity under fire undoubtedly impressed General Worth and led him to select the Rangers to form part of his assault force on both days of the attacks against the fortified mountain strongpoints. In fact, the Rangers made up almost half of the assaulting elements on both days. The Rangers even earned the grudging respect of the proud infantry Regulars. James Greer notes that, "One of the men from the Fifth Infantry exclaimed to some of the Rangers, "Well, boys, we almost beat you!" [to the summit of Federation Hill] and he pulled a piece of chalk from his pocket and wrote on one of the cannon, "Texas Rangers and Fifth Infantry."[26]

The Rangers' accurate rifle fire almost certainly helped the assault forces gain the heights whereupon the firepower of their pistols also conferred a marked advantage on the attackers. The hard won combat experience of the Texans' leaders also helped turn the tide of battle and reduce friendly casualties; Hays' innovative plan to lure the Mexican defenders from the security of the Bishop's Palace proved exceedingly effective. The Rangers contributed much to the tactical success of Worth's Division in the attacks against Federation and Independence Hills and proved themselves to be effective dismounted fighters. Moreover, the Rangers incurred no accusations of improprieties or innuendos of misdeeds during this phase of the battle, most likely because all of their attention was focused on winning the fights at hand.

Capturing Monterey

On Wednesday, 23 September, both wings of Taylor's army prepared to assault the city, but curiously without coordination. On the east, Taylor sent forth Quitman's brigade of Volunteers (part of General Butler's Third

Division) to probe the city's defenses. Finding some of the outlying forts abandoned the men entered the city proper until they met resistance. At this point General Taylor ordered forward Wood's Second Texas (dismounted) and two regiments of Regulars. The Texans soon began leading the attack in the east fighting street by street and house by house. Although these men likely did not take part in the street fights during the capture of Bexar (now known as San Antonio in 1835) and Mier (in 1842) they certainly benefited from the stories of the western Rangers' combat experience.[27] One observer in Quitman's brigade, T. B. Thorpe, recalled,

> It was a terrible sight, even compared to all those exhibited in the two days of sanguinary battle of Monterrey, to witness the Texans; adopting their own mode of fighting, they soon broke into the shut up houses, scaled walls, and appeared on the housetops. Whenever a Mexican displayed himself, the deadly fire of the rifle brought him down.[28]

The Rangers of the Second Texas, finally receiving their chance to fight, took to their work with relish and made steady progress into the town.

Around ten o'clock General Worth heard the sound of firing from the other side of the city and "he inferred that Taylor was now conducting the main attack, that the roar of the guns was tantamount to an order for cooperation, and that Taylor's instructions had either been captured or delayed in transit."[29] Shortly thereafter Colonel Hays received a courier from General Worth with orders directing him to dismount his regiment and join the upcoming attack from the west. Hays writes,

On the afternoon of the 23rd, when Gen. Worth led his division from the Bishop's Palace into the city, I proceeded under his orders with my entire command (save about sixty men who were engaged in scouting and other special duties) consisting of about 400 men to the church where he had established his batteries.
There [I] divided my command, Lt Col. Walker, commanding the left wing, proceeded toward the enemy's batteries by Iturbide Street.[30]

Hays led a force of Regulars and Rangers in an attack down Calle de Monterrey. Walker, also leading a mixed force, paralleled him along Calle de Iturbide.
Soon each column began conducting combined arms type attacks with infantry forces penetrating houses and fighting through them, snipers firing from rooftops to suppress enemy marksmen, and the artillery sweeping the streets with charges of canister. Hays' Rangers on the west and Wood's Rangers on the east used axes and crow bars to break holes in the adobe walls of the buildings sometimes firing blindly into the holes hoping to hit the Mexican defenders and sometime hurling in lit artillery shells as crude hand grenades. Upon seizing the ground floor of a house or building, the attackers quickly moved to the roof, cleared it, and began engaging any exposed Mexicans with accurate and deadly rifle fire to support the movement to the next building. A participant in the battle wrote, "When the report of a Texas rifle was heard, it was safe to bet a bullet had been bloodied."[31] James Greer continues,

A defender fought stubbornly and bravely, but if he showed a hand at a loophole, he became a cripple. Some of the Rangers watched the embrasures; when these darkened against the clear sky, rifles cracked, and light filled the embrasures again. If a Mexican raised his head above a parapet, a rifle ball pierced it. The well aimed rifles finally drained the enemy's spirit of resistance.[32]

Both groups of Rangers were displaying, and teaching their Regular and Volunteer counterparts, a new mode of fighting; one that greatly reduced friendly casualties while wreaking havoc on the Mexican defenders. These tactics stood in bold contrast to the massed infantry attacks across open ground that had been employed only two days prior at such dreadful cost. Despite the advantages of being on the defensive and enjoying interior lines, the Mexicans were unable to withstand the multi-pronged, three dimensional attack of the Texas Rangers and continually gave ground. By late afternoon, the two wings of Taylor's army had penetrated to within a block of the Central Plaza on either side. Inexplicably, Taylor ordered the eastern assault force to withdraw. The Mexican defenders soon redoubled their efforts against Hays' men on the west, but the Rangers and Regulars held on to the day's gains with Walker's Rangers spending the night in the city.

As day broke on the 24th, the Rangers and the Regulars again took up the fight. Hays soon led his men back into the city from the outskirts where they had spent the night caring for their horses and standing guard.[33] Soon the troops from the east joined the fight but at about ten o'clock the order came to cease fire. "Hays sat with his men from ten until five o'clock in the broiling sun, only eight yards from the cathedral and within a few hours of securing an unconditional surrender."[34]

However close the Rangers may have been from conquering the city, Zachary Taylor had had enough and after some bargaining accepted the surrender of the garrison but on very favorable terms; Ampudia's men would be allowed to leave the city with a battery of field artillery, twenty one rounds of ammunition, and his cavalry's horses. Even more shocking for the Texans and Taylor's superiors in Washington, Ampudia agreed to retire beyond the Rinconda pass and in return Taylor agreed not to advance past Monterey for eight weeks.[35]

Hardly the terms of surrender that a beaten force would expect, but an analysis of the casualties Taylor's army had suffered in its attacks on Monterey may help explain the generous terms. James Greer notes that, "Taylor's loss in killed and wounded was approximately eight hundred, while Worth's, whose men advanced according to orders, nonhaphazardly, was about seventy."[36] Official losses of nearly nine hundred men in just four days of fighting out of force of six thousand had clearly given Taylor pause (some estimates place the casualty figures higher).[37] His army could not sustain such losses and hope to continue its drive toward Mexico City. While these considerations, and the need to rest and refit his weary troops, certainly would have weighed on Taylor's decision to continue the fight, they in no way explain why he granted such overly generous terms to the Mexican commander; he never needed to know Taylor's dilemma and probably faced a worse set of conditions on his own side. Nevertheless, the Mexican commander signed the surrender in the early morning hours of 25 September bringing to a close the battle of Monterey.[38]

The Texas Rangers made one of their most significant contributions to the war in this phase of the battle. No other unit of the American army had combat experience fighting in cities. In fact, only the Regulars would have had any combat experience at all before the war, all of it against Indians in unconventional battles in the open or against Indian villages. Combat among the stone houses and brick streets of Monterey conferred a much greater advantage on the defender than the cloth or buffalo hide tepees of the Indian villages. Here the Texans excelled. They not only took to the street fighting with a boldness that surprised the Mexicans, they taught Taylor's army how to fight in an urban environment. Without the benefit of the Rangers' experience, Taylor's army may not have succeeded in capturing Monterey, and if it had, the cost in lives certainly would have been much higher. The tactical contributions of the Texas Rangers in the urban fight for Monterey made the difference between compelling a quick Mexican surrender and a long and bloody stalemate that might have changed the course of the war.

Garrisoning Monterey

Taylor's surrender terms and truce generated mixed feelings among his troops. Some welcomed the end of the fighting and thought it a prudent move to prevent further bloodshed. Others, mainly the Texas Rangers, considered it folly and thought that victory had been snatched from their grasp yet again by the cunning Mexicans. Samuel C. Reid of Hays' Regiment wrote, "A burst of indignation and angry discontent was manifested on every side, . . . The Texians were maddened with disappointment. Old Rough and Ready [General Taylor] had committed a great blunder, with no justifiable excuse."[39] Major Luther Giddings of the

First Ohio Regiment, a less sympathetic observer, wrote that,

> The fault finders in our army were chiefly the Texans. On the night of the 23rd of September they had obtained possession of the highest houses in the vicinity of the great plaza, and, unsated with slaughter, they but waited for the morning to avenge signally the hoarded wrongs suffered during their long war for independence. The capitulation of the 24th, of course, disappointed all their sweet and long cherished hopes of vengeance.[40]

However, Giddings misses an important aspect of the Texans' experience with Mexican commanders; honorable surrenders are only valuable if your adversary adheres to the terms of the agreement. William "Bigfoot" Wallace, second in command of Gillespie's company, stated that, "whenever [the Mexicans] hoisted the white flag and succeeded in persuading the Americans to 'parley,' they invariably got the better of them in one way or other."[41] The Texans surely remembered Santa Anna's duplicity in renouncing the terms of his surrender at San Jacinto in 1836; once safely across the Rio Grande he quickly forgot the stipulations of his release. Many of the men in Hays' command, including Lieutenant Colonel Samuel Walker, his second in command, had survived the fight for Mier in 1842 in which Colonel Fisher had surrendered his men to General Ampudia. Many of these men undoubtedly wished to avenge themselves upon Ampudia for the indignity of their surrender at Mier and the subsequent murder of many of the prisoners in the black bean incident. The Texans also likely realized that someone would have to fight these same troops again, as Taylor later did at Buena Vista.

In that battle the Mexicans again used a flag of truce to gain advantage on the battlefield.

Like it or not, the battle was over and the job the Texans came to do had been done. They had enlisted as three month volunteers and agreed to accept another term in order to join the fight for Monterey, but with the fighting now over they began to chafe at army life and yearned to return to their homes. Few regulars or Volunteers were sorry to see them go. The same men who had relied on the Rangers in combat and lauded their effectiveness in battle now wished them a speedy departure. Zachary Taylor wrote on 28 September that, "The General feels assured that every individual in the command unites with him in admiration of the distinguished gallantry and conduct of Colonel Hays and his noble band of Texian volunteers, hereafter they and we are brothers, and we can desire no better guarantee of success than by their association."[42]

On 6 October, just twelve days after the end of the battle Taylor wrote of the Rangers, ". . . with their departure we may look for a restoration of quiet and good order in Monterey, for I regret to report that some shameful atrocities have been perpetrated by them since the capitulation of the town."[43] The incidents Taylor wrote of certainly did not involve the whole command yet he painted all Rangers with the same brush despite the actions of their commanders. Colonel Hays reacted swiftly to the killing of a Mexican lancer some days after the end of hostilities, likely one of the atrocities referred to by Taylor. Hays, nearby the scene when he heard a shot, immediately investigated. He found one of his men near the scene of the killing and challenged him, examining his pistol, which had been fired recently. The man denied any knowledge of the shooting whereupon Hays had him arrested and turned him over to the proper military authorities.[44] Yet herein lay one of the enduring problems of the Mexican War, no formal authority existed with which the army could punish troops for violation that would have fallen under the jurisdiction of civilian courts in the United States.

Taylor lacked formal authority and he was unwilling to assume the informal authority necessary to deal with such gross violations of the law as murder, rape, and serious theft. Instead, Taylor wrote to Secretary of War Marcy for guidance, what he received was the recommendation that the man be sent from the army since the crime was not specifically listed in the Articles of War.[45] So rather than deal effectively with the problem Taylor merely wished it away by granting the Texas Rangers their discharges on 30 September, disbanding the two regiments, and looking "for a restoration of quiet and good order in Monterey."[46] It was not to be. As David Lavender notes,

> Other riotous volunteers, however, took their places. A group of men apparently from a Kentucky regiment broke into a residence in the Monterrey suburbs, threw out the husband, and raped his wife. Soon after that a Kentuckian was found dead, his throat slashed. In the following days other persons, both Mexican and volunteers, were wounded or killed as a result of the initial crime. Victims included a twelve year old Mexican boy, who was shot in the leg."[47]

Rather than enforcing commonly accepted rules of conduct and holding his subordinates accountable, Taylor seemed content to castigate entire units and the only action he took was to vent his frustrations in letters to friends and colleagues back home. It is noteworthy that other commanders did find ways to

deal with the lack of formal law enforcement authority. Jack Bauer notes that,
> It would have been difficult for any commander of a force including significant numbers of poorly disciplined volunteers to prevent these collisions, but other commanders, notably Wool and Scott, devised methods of holding such incidents to a minimum.[48]

One successful method was to keep the Texans on the trail and out of the towns; idle Texans proved to be threat to Mexicans and other soldiers.

The criminal actions of some individuals during the garrisoning of Monterey did much to tarnish the reputation of the Texas Rangers and besmirched their hard won battlefield accolades. However, as noted earlier such incidents did not end with the departure of the Rangers and therefore although their indiscipline surely caused Taylor problems they were not the sole cause of such problems. Taylor's inaction granted a form of tacit approval of such acts. Regardless of the problems they caused, Taylor soon found himself in need of the skills only the Texans could provide. He would call on them again to serve as the eyes and ears of his army and to engage in a bitter counter-guerilla fight to protect his extended lines of supply and communications. He might have disliked their lawlessness and eschewed their methods, but he was content to use them for his most dangerous and dirty tasks.

Indispensable in combat and intolerable in peace, the Texans made their way back to the Rio Grande border. Before they departed Monterey, Taylor elicited a promise from Ben McCulloch to recruit another spy company and return to duty with the army if hostilities resumed.[49] McCulloch did not have long to wait.

CHAPTER 6 - TAYLOR'S CAMPAIGN: THE BATTLE OF BUENA VISTA

To Buena Vista

When the news of Taylor's victory at Monterey reached Washington on 11 October 1846, President James K. Polk and Secretary of War William L. Marcy privately criticized the terms of surrender and the armistice granted by Taylor. As the country celebrated Taylor's success Polk wrote in his diary that, "He [Taylor] had the enemy in his power & should have taken them prisoners . . . and preserved the advantage he had obtained by pushing on without delay."[1] The Secretary of War quickly wrote Taylor a letter ordering the immediate termination of the armistice.

The order had little effect on Taylor, the requisite time for messages to travel to Washington and back meant that he did not receive Marcy's order until 2 November, by that time five weeks of the eight week armistice had already elapsed.[2] It is unlikely that Taylor would have initiated new combat operations prior to the end of the eight weeks armistice anyway as he needed time to rest and refit his depleted forces. Taylor soon complied with his orders to end the armistice when he sent Santa Anna a letter notifying him that the armistice was to end on 13 November. Soon after the end of the truce Taylor ordered General Worth's Regulars forward to Saltillo. On the 16th, Worth occupied the town.[3] As Taylor's army inched forward, the strategy in Washington shifted away from Taylor's theater of war and towards an invasion of Central Mexico.

Based on Taylor's reports, the President and the Secretary of War determined that a march on Mexico

City by way of the northern route through Monterey, Saltillo, and San Luis Potosi was not feasible due to the vast expanse of desert to be crossed. Therefore, the planners determined to attack Mexico City by way of the Gulf coast with a landing at Vera Cruz. General Winfield Scott, the Army's senior general, would command the expedition. To man his operations, General Scott ordered the majority of Taylor's forces detached from Taylor's command in the north and assigned to Scott to form a new army.

Lieutenant John A Richey carried the secret orders, dated 13 January 1847, for the reallocation of forces.[4] Taylor was to lose some nine thousand men: four thousand Regular Infantry, four thousand Volunteer Infantry, plus a thousand mounted troops, and some artillery batteries.[5] Unfortunately, Lieutenant Richey never delivered the orders, he became separated from his Dragoon escorts in a small Mexican village near Linares and was captured, tortured, and killed.[6] The dispatches Richey carried soon made their way into the hands of Santa Anna who immediately sensed an approaching opportunity to attack and destroy Taylor's weakened force. Duplicate orders soon reached Taylor and, despite whatever reluctance he might have had, he sent the units on their way back towards the Texas border to join Scott's army preparing for a new campaign in Central Mexico.

Taylor's shrunken army, which now consisted of only about five thousand inexperienced volunteers and some five hundred Regulars, mostly artillerymen, lay dangerously exposed deep in enemy country and far from its bases of supplies. Luckily for Taylor and his small band of freshly recruited volunteers, Brigadier General John E. Wool's veteran army had arrived a few weeks earlier with close to three thousand men, many of them Regulars.[7] With the addition of Wool's troops,

Taylor's force numbered about eight thousand men but the need to garrison Monterey, station troops along his lines of supply, and illness all reduced the numbers of men he would be able to count on in a fight.

Santa Anna's army, including the forces of Ampudia that had escaped destruction at Monterey, gathered strength at San Luis Potosí for the strike against Taylor. The Mexican forces, however, far outnumbered the Americans: more than twenty thousand troops, including about 6,700 cavalry, and all the irregulars Santa Anna could lure to the region with promises of an easy victory and plenty of looting.[8] Santa Anna planned to march his men across the vast deserts between San Luis Potosí and Saltillo and destroy Taylor's small force before turning toward the coast to defeat Scott's army. David Lavender explains,

> Santa Anna was so confident of this [a victory over Taylor] that he already had made preparations to decimate the fleeing Americans. He ordered J. V. Miñon to take position with his lancers in Palomas Pass, east of Saltillo, so that they could fall on the fugitives streaming north, and he appealed for guerillas from as far away as Parras and Monclova to hurry to the Saltillo plain and help with the slaughter.[9]

Santa Anna's vast army departed San Luis Potosí on 27 January 1847.[10] The stage was almost set for the climactic battle of the northern theater of the war.

Battle of Buena Vista

As early as 30 November 1846, Ben McCulloch recognized that the war in the north was likely to begin anew.[11] He soon set about recruiting another company of Rangers from among his fellow citizens of Gonzales, Texas and reported for duty at Taylor's headquarters at Monterey on 31 January 1847.[12]

McCulloch's men could not have arrived at a better time. Taylor's force, only 4,759 strong (the remainder was either strung out between Saltillo and the Texas border or unfit for duty due to illness), sorely lacked good intelligence on the location of Santa Anna's much larger army.[13] On 22 January, an American reconnaissance force numbering about seventy men was surprised by 500 Mexican lancers and forced to surrender. Mexican lancers captured another patrol of Kentucky cavalry on the 27th. By late January, Taylor desperately needed solid intelligence on the size and location of Santa Anna's army. He suspected the enemy to be moving towards him from the south, but he did not know how large a formation he was facing, and when and from what direction it might attack. Upon his arrival at Monterey, McCulloch found that Taylor and his army were gone so he pressed on to Saltillo (reacting to alarms sent by Worth, and later Wool, Taylor had moved his headquarters forward to Saltillo in late January).

McCulloch arrived at Saltillo on 4 February and met with Taylor to offer the services of his twenty seven men. McCulloch proposed that he and his troops would serve for six months to be paid as regular soldiers or they would serve until the end of the upcoming battle in exchange for food for themselves and their mounts. Taylor replied that the men would only be accepted if they enlisted for the duration of the war. The Rangers demurred because, knowing that several earlier scouting parties had been captured, they were in a position to bargain. Taylor needed their unique expertise so the Rangers held out for the terms they wanted. As McCulloch noted, "the General was in a tight place and the services very hazardous in as much as all the reconnoitering detachments sent out had been captured by the enemy."[14] Taylor soon relented and the company was mustered in for six months as McCulloch's Company, Texas Mounted Volunteers (Spies).[15]

On 5 February, Taylor advanced his men seventeen miles south of Saltillo to Agua Nueva, in part to restore the confidence of his green troops, a confidence shaken by the uncertainty surrounding Santa Anna's whereabouts and the capture of the scouting parties.[16] McCulloch's men could do little to restore the fighting spirit of Taylor's volunteers, but the Rangers knew how to scout in enemy territory without being captured.

On the night of 16 February 1847, Ben McCulloch departed on his first scout of this second phase of his Mexican War service. Accompanied by sixteen of his Rangers, McCulloch led the party fifteen miles south of the new American positions Agua Nueva to Rancho La Encarnación (see figure 3).[17] As Walter Prescott Webb notes, "Reports were constantly coming in [to Taylor] that Santa Anna was advancing with 20,000 men to fall on Taylor's raw troops, and this scout was for the purpose of ascertaining the truth."[18] McCulloch's men captured a Mexican picket outside the town who denied that he was part of Santa Anna's army. On approaching closer to the town, the Rangers alerted another picket who fled into the night.

The Rangers next encountered a line of Mexican cavalry some four hundred yards from the town. "Quien vive?" broke the silence, followed by a volley from the Mexicans. McCulloch answered by ordering an immediate charge. McCulloch wrote that only about six of his men could comply with the order to charge, the startled horses of the rest distracted their riders.

"However, by the discharge of a few guns and pistols in their faces and some mighty tall yells, they were put to flight." That was enough for McCulloch, who rightly determined that "if we could not make them run, we must ourselves, as both our orders and their numbers cautioned us against fighting."[19] Showing a level of prudence lost on the commanders of previous reconnaissance patrols, McCulloch retired to render his report to Taylor.[20] Walter Prescott Webb adds that, "The Rangers returned to headquarters before day, having triumphed where others had repeatedly failed."[21]

Still lacking accurate intelligence, Taylor sent forth a second, larger reconnaissance party on 20 February. The force, under the command of Lieutenant Colonel Charles A. May, consisted of almost all of Taylor's remaining Dragoons (some 400 in all) plus two six pound artillery pieces. Taylor, having a well founded faith in McCulloch and realizing the unique skills of his Spy Company, wisely ordered him to accompany May's Dragoons. McCulloch asked the Commanding General if he planned to send anyone towards Encarnación. When Taylor said no, McCulloch reiterated that he thought the enemy he had skirmished with days prior were part of a larger Mexican force and won Taylor's approval to scout toward Encarnación. McCulloch's intuition would prove to be fortuitous for the fate of Taylor's army.

McCulloch and a hand picked force of five Rangers (Lieutenant Fielding Alston, a Ranger sergeant, three Ranger privates, and a volunteer Lieutenant from the Kentucky Infantry) set out on the afternoon of 20 February along with May's Dragoons.[22] Five or six miles from town the two groups parted ways; May's Dragoons headed east to reconnoiter the rancho of La Hedionda about sixteen miles east of Agua Nueva, while McCulloch's Rangers turned south to investigate La Encarnación. Eight miles south of Agua Nueva, the Rangers encountered a Mexican deserter named Valdez who claimed that Santa Anna was at Encarnación with his entire army of 20,000 men. McCulloch handed the man over to the American pickets with orders to have him taken to Taylor's headquarters and then led his men southward to see for themselves.

The Rangers spotted the fires from Santa Anna's camp five miles from Encarnación. McCulloch suspected that the enemy army was preparing to advance in the morning because the soldiers were up late cooking rations. He quickly decided to split his force in order to ensure that the crucial information got back to Taylor. Placing Lieutenant Alston in command of the detachment, McCulloch instructed him to return to Taylor's camp by the fastest possible route and inform the general that Santa Anna's army had been found. Meanwhile, McCulloch, accompanied by Sergeant William S. Phillips, decided to stay until the dawn to "take a daylight view of the enemy."[24] His men considered staying behind "to be extremely hazardous". McCulloch himself later admitted that it was "indeed a risky affair."[25] That said, McCulloch trusted his own abilities and knew that the more information he could bring back the better the American's chances would be.[26]

McCulloch and Phillips, having seen off the detachment carrying the vital news back to Taylor, set off to determine the size of the enemy camp. The Rangers spent a cold, sleepless night avoiding the Mexican pickets and trying not to get caught. The two men carefully scouted the outline of the camp and determined it to be about one mile long and one quarter mile wide. After estimating the size of the camp, McCulloch and Phillips climbed a hill and settled in to await the dawn.[27]

As day broke, the Mexican soldiers lit their warming fires, but the smoke from the green wood they used soon blanketed the camp, obscuring the Rangers' view. However, McCulloch had seen enough, it was time to make their way back to friendly lines. But with the daylight, McCulloch and Phillips realized the full danger of their position; two Mexican pickets flanked their position only some four hundred yards apart. McCulloch remarked that "the chances were against us."[28] Fortunately for the Rangers the Mexican pickets mistook the Texans for compatriots hunting stray horses and allowed them to pass. Yet the danger was far from over, the Rangers still had to pass the outer line of Mexican pickets at Tank Lavaca some twelve miles north of Encarnación.[29]

On nearing the outer picket line, McCulloch and Phillips climbed a rise and settled in to wait and see if the Mexicans would retire. At about 11:00 A.M. the Rangers spotted dust rising to south, a sure sign that Santa Anna's army was on the move, yet the pickets showed no sign of withdrawing. Thomas Cutrer writes that, "McCulloch was painfully aware that Alston's party may have been killed or captured, and should Taylor's army be surprised at Agua Nueva, defeat was inevitable. No option remained but to attempt to pass."[30] The Rangers skirted the hillside, in view of the Mexican pickets, but apparently unnoticed, and after passing Tank Lavaca they spurred their horses for the American lines.

Arriving at the American positions McCulloch found them abandoned; Lieutenant Alston's party had already delivered the warning to Taylor and he had withdrawn his army from the exposed plain of Agua Nueva to the more easily defensible narrows of Angostura pass, near a *hacienda* (ranch house) known as Buena Vista, some fourteen miles back toward Saltillo. This location conferred several advantages on Taylor's small force: it was bounded on both sides by high mountains so his army could not be easily flanked; the main road narrowed sharply so it could be effectively blocked; and the plateaus to the left flank were crisscrossed with ravines and defiles which would negate the effectiveness of the Mexican lancers. McCulloch and Phillips continued north and at about 4:00 P.M. they entered the new American lines. McCulloch immediately reported to Taylor's headquarters. General Taylor, upon receiving McCulloch's account of the enemy disposition, remarked, "Very well, Major, that's all I wanted to know. I am glad they did not catch you."[31]

A patrol of McCulloch's Rangers delivered the final warning on the morning of 22 February 1847. A small party of Rangers, riding south to locate the enemy, exchanged fire with the advance guard of Santa Anna's army and quickly withdrew to notify the commanding general. Taylor rapidly deployed his army and awaited the arrival of the enemy. Santa Anna's army, now numbering only some fifteen thousand after its losses crossing the wasteland between San Luis Potosí and Agua Nueva, still outnumbered Taylor by nearly three to one. Upon his arrival, Santa Anna courteously offered Taylor the opportunity to surrender and avoid "catastrophe," but the American commander declined.[32]

Two days of fierce battle followed in which the American fended off assault after assault by the Mexican infantry and lancers. As in the first battles of the war, the American six pound "flying" artillery batteries proved their worth in battle.[33] Repeatedly during the two days of fighting the artillery blunted attacks and steadied the wavering ranks of the green volunteer regiments. McCulloch's Rangers did take part in the battle as both dismounted infantry and regular cavalry, but their small numbers made a minimal impact on the course of the conflict.[34] Another company of Texans also fought at Buena Vista. A unit of Texas infantry that Taylor lists in his report as "Captain Conner's company of Texas volunteers" fought alongside the Second Illinois Regiment, but also made only a small impact on the battle. The major contribution of the Texans came earlier, in locating the enemy and giving Taylor the time to deploy for battle. Yet the outnumbered Americans needed every man and every gun they could muster, so the Texans, Infantry and Rangers, again fought in a conventional battle.

When the smoke cleared on the morning of the 24th, Taylor's army rejoiced; the Mexican army was gone. Zachary Taylor had won his second remarkable victory of the war and the ensuing fame launched him on an easy road to the White House. After the fighting, McCulloch requested and was granted leave. He departed on 5 March and left command of the company to Lieutenant Alston. The company remained in Mexico until late May when it was mustered out of service at the end of its six month enlistment.[35]

The contributions of McCulloch's Rangers during this phase of the war are hard to overstate. Although few in number, they possessed a wealth of experience that they put to immediate use to gather and report information that had previously eluded all other reconnaissance units sent forth by Taylor. The Rangers accomplished what no other force could do, they found Santa Anna's army, infiltrated its lines, and returned with information that directly contributed to the success, and even the survival, of the American army.

Webb succinctly summarizes the operation when he writes,

> The regulars came back with rumors of an approaching army, which was nothing new; the Rangers returned only after entering the Mexican's camp and ascertaining for themselves the enemy's numbers and condition. The four hundred dragoons returned with a loss of a lieutenant and private captured; the seven Texans returned in two separate parties and without loss.[36]

Zachary Taylor underplays the importance of the Rangers' contribution when he writes the he and his army were "greatly indebted" to McCulloch and his men and that they "rendered us much good service as spies. The intelligence which they brought caused us to leave the plains of Agua Nueva for a very strong and advantageous position."[37] It would have been closer to the truth to say that McCulloch and his scouts had saved the army, but few commanding generals would ever admit so embarrassing a detail. Still, this was high praise from the normally reserved Taylor.

In this action, the Rangers' came closer to delivering service of "inestimable value" than at almost any other time during the war. As Webb wrote, "Their acts often had a strategic value that was inestimable, upon which the fate of an army, a battle, or even a campaign depended."[38] This sentence does not boast; one seemingly small reconnaissance action by the Texas Rangers had made a critical impact on the subsequent battle and the northern campaign. Had Santa Anna surprised Taylor's army on the open plains of Agua Nueva it is quite possible that the larger Mexican force would have defeated the Americans and the outcome of the war might have been very different indeed.

CHAPTER 7 - COUNTER-GUERILLA OPERATIONS

Counter-Guerilla Operations in Northern Mexico

The war in the North did not end with Taylor's victory at Buena Vista; rather it continued as a dirty guerilla war along his extended lines of supply. This type of irregular warfare was not new to the northern theater. Many units moving from the Texas Border to the interior had faced Mexican bandits, lancers, and guerilla bands under the likes of Canales and Seguin, but as Taylor's army fought for control of Monterey, the war to maintain his communications and supply link with the United States took a decided turn for the worse.

On 23 February 1847, as Taylor's army fought for its life at Buena Vista, a strong force of irregular cavalry (part lancers and part bandits) seized an American supply train about nine miles from the village of Marin.[1] The Mexicans executed and mutilated the fifty teamsters, took the infantry escort prisoner and burned what they could not carry away with them.[2] Colonel Samuel R. Curtis, of the 3rd Ohio Regiment, arriving at the scene on 15 March describes the carnage,

> The bodies are strewn from this place two or three miles. These bodies are the wagoners and men under command of Lieut. Barbour attacked on the 23rd February. They were attacked on a side hill, and the massacre continued throughout the entire length of the train.[3]

Major Luther Giddings, of the First Ohio, passed through some time later and wrote that the road between Camargo and Monterey was "dotted with the skeletons of men and animals. Roofless and ruined ranchos, and many a dark and smouldering [sic] heap of ashes, told the disasters."[4]

Colonel Curtis realized the danger of such guerilla activity along his lines of supply even before seeing the devastation for himself on the 15th. In his capacity as the commander of the American garrison at Camargo he wrote the Governor of Texas on 2 March 1847 that,

> All communication has for several days been cut off between this place [Camargo] and General Taylor's Head Quarters [at Monterey]. Our last communication is dated the 21st. Ult. [of February], and the General was then threatened by a large army in front, and a very considerable force in his rear.
>
> Private communications informs us, that Santa Anna had demanded a surrender, and General Taylor had replied to him to come and take him. Since that date all is doubt, darkness, rumor. It is certain the General is besieged, and that too, by a large force of Cavalry in his rear.
>
> I believe the occasion requires a large force to raise the siege, and therefore request you to call out two thousand mounted men. As far as possible, they should procure arms and ammunition, and repair to this point as fast as companies can be organized and equipped. The call might be for four month's men.[5]

Colonel Curtis' letter triggered the entry of the third significant group of Texas Rangers to the northern theater of the Mexican War. These units fought a bitter counter-guerilla war, and although most served nobly, others committed depredations equal to those of their Mexican foes. Far from winning accolades in combat, all reaped only casualties and scorn for their efforts.

Major Michael Chevallie's Battalion, Texas Mounted Volunteers, three companies strong, responded to the call and quickly departed San Antonio for Camargo. This battalion was organized in November 1846 (shortly after the battle of Monterey) but had not yet been called forward into Mexico. Chevallie's Battalion originally claimed only three companies, but it later gained another two in mid June 1847. Although Chevallie commanded fewer companies than the earlier First Texas Mounted Volunteers, each company was at or over its full authorized strength of one hundred men and thus its total numbers rivaled those of Hays' Regiment.[6] Moreover, many of the men and officers of the battalion had combat experience gained at Monterey.

Also responding to Colonel Curtis' plea for immediate assistance was Captain Mabry B. Gray's company from Corpus Christi. Although not officially part of Chevallie's Battalion, Gray's men operated in the same areas during the same time periods and therefore their actions and reputations are intertwined. "Mustang" Gray's company arrived at Camargo first and Colonel Curtis soon ordered them to convoy escort duty along the road between Monterey and Camargo. It was a fateful decision. Gray carried with him a reputation for excess (evidenced by his nickname) and was known for his merciless treatment of Mexicans. In 1840, Gray's entire family had been slaughtered by Mexican raiders under Canales, and he had been accused of the murder of several Mexicans in 1842 near Goliad Texas, but was never arrested.[7] Clearly this was not a man who could be expected to expend much effort to distinguish Mexican guerilla raider from Mexican non-combatant villager, as events would soon show.

On 20 May, a large supply convoy departed Camargo; one hundred loaded wagons, five hundred men, some Dragoons, and Gray's company of Rangers.[8] Major Giddings' unit (the First Ohio Volunteers) accompanied the supply train as it made its way through the heart of the contested area between Camargo and Monterey. As they passed by the scene of the wagon train massacre outside Marin, Giddings notes that,

> There Captain Gray and his Rangers separated from the command, for the purpose, as was said, of obtaining forage. The column pursued its march a few miles farther, and encamped for the night at the stream near Marin. I was informed that one of the Texans had recognized a brother among the decaying remains of mortality in the valley, and with tears of grief and rage, had insisted upon avenging his death in the blood of the first Mexicans they encountered.[9]

The vengeance of Gray's men was swift and indiscriminate; they murdered almost the entire male population of a nearby ranch, some twenty four men.[10] Because the local inhabitants feared for their lives none would identify the perpetrators, and so Gray again escaped justice. Rather than search for those responsible for the massacre of the American teamsters, these men vented their hate and frustration on the nearest group of Mexicans they could find, guilt mattered not.

Luckily for Taylor (and the Mexican populace), Chevallie's battalion arrived for service in April and

May 1847, and Gray's company was mustered out in July.[11] Regardless of the fact that new Ranger units, under new leadership, arrived to carry on the counter-guerilla fight, Gray's reprisal further damaged Taylor's opinion of the Texas Rangers. He still required their services, but he trusted them and their leaders less and less.

As the counter-guerilla war dragged on and on, the new Ranger leadership found itself tested by both the Mexican irregulars and their American superiors, even as they scored some notable successes. In August, Major Chevallie quarreled with General Wool and resigned his command.[12] Captain Walter P. Lane, who later wrote a detailed account of his experiences, succeeded him as commander of the Battalion. The change in command also highlights the fact that the senior leadership of Texas Rangers, men like Hays, Walker, McCulloch, and now Chevallie, were absent from this phase of the war in the north.

Upon reporting for duty at Taylor's headquarters in Monterey, Lane received orders to "go down to Cerralvo and capture or kill a band of guerila's [sic] there under Juan Flores."[13] Flores and his men were suspected of being the actual persons responsible for the killing of the American teamsters. Lane took a portion of his command and scouted the area surrounding Cerralvo. The Rangers soon found a guerilla camp of about thirty men. As Lane recalls, they "charged into them, killing or wounding about eight or ten of them. The balance stampeded in every direction through the chaparral [dense brush] and we were unable to capture them."[14]

Lane, thinking it unlikely he would be able to locate any members of the now dispersed band because his men could not recognize any of them, prepared to return to Monterey. Before the Rangers left, two

Mexicans cautiously approached the Ranger camp and agreed to lead the men to a nearby village and identify Juan Flores.[15] Lane and his men entered the village, found Flores hiding in a bed, and captured him. The Rangers took Flores to Cerralvo, held a trial, found him guilty and shot him the following day. Upon reporting these actions to General Taylor, Lane recounts that, "he expressed himself well pleased with my mission, stating it would be a death blow to guerillas in that part of the country."[16]

Taylor next sent Lane's Rangers into the interior of Mexico to confirm a report that General José Urrea (whom Lane erroneously refers to in his accounts as Gurea) was massing troops at the town of Madelina. Lane agreed to depart the following day with three hundred men, but he also recalls some trepidation at the order,

> He [Taylor] certainly showed very little consideration for our safety in sending so small a force into a hostile country, so far from succor or supply; for, had Gurea [sic] been there, as we heard, with ten thousand men, very few of us would have escaped to give him the information; all of which, I was aware, would not have troubled Gen. Taylor much, as he had a queer opinion of Texas troops. For he said to an officer, one day: "On the day of battle, I am glad to have Texas soldiers with me, for they are brave and gallant; but I never want to see them before or afterwards, for they are too hard to control."[17]

Lane led his men on the mission despite these concerns.

Upon nearing Madelina, Lane issued orders to his men concerning the use of deadly force, the only such order found in the historical records of the Texas Rangers' Mexican war service. Lane wrote that his men "were instructed, if they came across any armed Mexicans, to order their surrender, and fire upon them if they refused."[18] Given the nature of the war at this point and Lane's location deep inside Mexican territory, it seems a prudent order, yet the results of this order caused him more trouble with Taylor than the questionable trial and execution of Juan Flores.

Lane divided his men into three commands as they entered the city. Lieutenant Earland's squad was moving up a street when an armed Mexican galloped towards them. The men ordered him, in Spanish, to stop and surrender or they would kill him but he turned and fled. Ranger John Glandon pursued on a fast horse and quickly overtaking the man again ordered him in Spanish to halt or be killed. When the man showed no signs of compliance, Glandon shot and killed him and seized his horse.[19] The Rangers returned to Taylor's headquarters several days later to report.

Lane was shocked at Taylor's demeanor upon the return of the command. He writes that, "instead of the kind and affable manner he always received me, he commenced abusing my command as a set of robbers and cut throats."[20] Taylor had received a letter from the governor of Madelina by express rider decrying the Rangers' actions there and accusing them of the murdering the fleeing man in cold blood, the taking of provisions and forage without pay, and conduct unbecoming United States soldiers. Taylor chose to believe the mayor of an enemy town during wartime over his own subordinate officer! He ordered Lane to immediately surrender Glandon, whom Taylor called "the murderer," and have him brought to Taylor's headquarters in irons. Lane refused. When Taylor ordered Lane arrested, Lane fled to his command.

Upon his arrival at the Ranger camp, Lane told Glandon to "skip" for San Antonio.[21]

Taylor's Adjutant, Lieutenant Colonel William W. S. Bliss, soon arrived at the Rangers' camp with orders to arrest Lane. As the men talked, Lane explained his actions at Madelina and sent for Lieutenant Shackelford (one of Taylor's Regular officers) who verified Lane's account of the incident. Bliss informed Taylor and, as Lane writes, "after a few days, old 'Rough and Ready' sent for me, relieved me from arrest, and made a grumbling kind of apology that he had been too hasty."[22]

The counter-guerilla war in the north continued in this manner for the next several months. The Mexicans attacked small convoys and killed stray groups of Americans; the Rangers hunted enemy guerillas and killed some; and Mexican civilians continued to accuse the Rangers of theft and plunder. When American authorities believed Mexican accounts of abuse at the hands of the Rangers, they sought to impose remedies, but many of these accusations were unfounded and some outright lies for personal gain.

Lane recounts receiving orders from General Wool to hand over several horses that local Mexicans accused the Rangers of stealing. When Lane accompanied the Mexicans to the corral for them to identify the horses in question, the men pointed out a horse belonging to one Lane's Ranger, a horse that had been mustered into United States service two years before! It seems the Mexican had learned to linger around the Rangers' corral and notice the various brands of the horses. They would then go to General Wool with witnesses and "prove" ownership, whereupon Wool would issue orders for the Rangers to relinquish the horses. Lane's response to the two men's attempt to steal his horse, long a capital crime on the frontier, showed a remarkable degree of restraint, especially for the supposedly bloodthirsty Rangers. Lane wrote that, "I, being averse to any hard feeling or difficulty, whispered to a few of my men to take the Mexicans down to ravine close by and settle the horse question with them; which they did, giving them about *one hundred apiece* [presumably punches or blows], the Mexicans barely escaping with their lives." (italics in original)[23] This apparently put an end to the Rangers' horse losses.

The Rangers' constant vigilance along the supply route, and their success in pursuing and punishing Mexican guerillas paid off in a sharp decline in the number of attacks. On 7 November 1847, Taylor declared the line between Camargo and Monterey "is now quite free of hostile parties."[24] However, Taylor kept Lane's Battalion in almost constant service until its discharge on 30 June 1848.[25]

This is a confused and poorly recorded era of the Texas Ranger's Mexican War service. The decentralized nature of counter-guerilla operations made them particularly difficult to document. The Rangers kept few records, and as few non-Rangers accompanied them on their missions there were very few observer accounts either. Space precludes an attempt to describe and analyze every counter-guerilla operation by each of the Ranger units, however, several important conclusions can be drawn. First, Chevallie's (and later Lane's) Battalion very likely committed no such atrocities. In fact, in several cases, Lane's men showed admirable restraint, discipline, and appreciation for orders seldom credited to the Rangers. Second, Taylor continued to blame units rather than the individual, warranted in the case of 'Mustang" Gray's company, but unwarranted in the case of Lane's Battalion, which muddied the historical record. Third, atrocities were very likely committed by Texas Rangers during this phase of the war, most notably Gray's company's killing of Mexican villagers near Marin.

However, other Volunteer units also committed massacres of similar scope; in early February 1847, the men of Colonel Archibald Yell's Arkansas Cavalry killed 20 to 30 Mexicans in a reprisal for the murder of one their men.[26] Taylor's adjutant, then Major William Bliss, had even gone so far as to issue Yell a written letter reprimanding his command for their atrocities several weeks prior on 4 January.[27] Yet participants at the time (Regular and Volunteer officers who observed the Rangers or in many cases criticized the Rangers' actions based only on rumors and without any firsthand knowledge) and many later historians, all branded the Texas Rangers "the worst offenders."[28] A clue to understanding why this is the case can be found by analyzing not only what Taylor said about the Rangers, but when he said it.[29]

Taylor's criticism of the Rangers is often cited, but it is seldom scrutinized. Taylor's letter of 16 June 1847 is an enlightening example when placed into context, a context sometimes overlooked. Here is what Taylor wrote to the Adjutant General,

> I deeply regret to report that many of the twelve months' volunteers in their route hence of the lower Rio Grande, have committed extensive depredations and outrages upon the peaceful inhabitants. There is scarcely a form of crime that has not been reported to me as committed by them; but they have passed beyond my reach, and even were they here, it would be next to impossible to detect the individuals who thus disgrace their colors and their country. Were it possible to rouse the

> Mexican people to resistance, no more effectual plan could be devised than the very one pursued by some of our volunteer regiments now about to be discharged.
>
> The volunteers for the war, so far, give an earnest of better conduct, with the exception of the companies of Texas horse. Of the infantry I have had little or no complaint; but the mounted men from Texas have scarcely made one expedition without unwarrantably killing a Mexican...The constant recurrence of such atrocities, which I have been reluctant to report to the department, is my motive for requesting that no more troops may be sent to this column from the State of Texas.[30]

Several points deserve to be made about this letter; first is the date when it was written, June 1847, after Monterey and after Buena Vista. The Texas Regiments of Hays and Woods departed Monterey in October 1846. McCulloch's men remained in Mexico even after his departure on 5 March 1847, but Taylor refers to "twelve months'" volunteers, while McCulloch's men enlisted for only six months. Therefore, it is unlikely that Taylor refers to Texas Rangers in his first paragraph.

Second, Taylor specifically refers to "companies" of Texas horse, this is quite likely a reference to Gray's company and other separate "Ranger" companies operating during the later counter-guerilla phase of the war and not, as some authors imply, an indictment of all Texas Rangers who served under Taylor's command during the war. Because Taylor singles out "companies" of Texas horse, it is possible that he meant to exclude Lane's Battalion of Texas Rangers from his rebuke, but that remains uncertain.

What is certain is the wording of the last sentence; Taylor requested "that no more troops may be sent to this column from the State of Texas." Far from the stern admonishment that this phrase first appears to be, it actually underscores Taylor's predicament with regard to the Rangers. He requested no more troops from Texas but he kept every unit from Texas in his service until the expiration of their terms of enlistment. The Rangers of Lane's Battalion and even those of Gray's company did perform a valuable service for Taylor's army, they checked, and finally ended the attacks of Mexican irregulars on Taylor's lines of supply. This phase of the war was costly for both sides; it cost the combatants much blood shed, Mexican guerilla and Texas Ranger; it costs the inhabitants lives and property lost, and it cost Taylor and the Rangers an indelible mark on their reputations. Overall, the Ranger's contribution in this phase must be assessed as mixed. They accomplished a task that no other unit of the American army was likely to have been able to do, but at a high price.

Counter-Guerilla Operations in Central Mexico

Though the Texas Rangers arrived late in the action, they also conducted counter-guerilla operations in support of the army's conventional forces in Central Mexico and, of course, executed some operations on their own accord. General Winfield Scott landed his army of 13,660 men at Vera Cruz, Mexico on 9 March 1847 and soon captured the town, the first amphibious landing in the history of the United States Army.[31] Scott's unbroken string of victories had just begun. He next defeated Santa Anna's army at Cerro Gordo and commenced his march on Mexico City. The battles of

Contreras, Churubusco, and Chapultapec followed and on 14 September 1847, Mexico City surrendered.[32] No Texas Ranger units took part in the capture of Mexico City. However, soon thereafter Samuel Walker, now serving as a Captain in the United States Army, arrived in command of a company of U.S. Mounted Rifles (Infantrymen who rode to battle on horses) and served as the advanced guard for General Joseph Lane's column as it moved from Vera Cruz to reinforce the occupation of the capital.[33] Robert Utley explains the situation,

> Scott's biggest challenge lay not in fighting hard contested battles but in keeping his army supplied. The National Road, linking the port of Vera Cruz with Mexico City, wound its way for 250 miles across three mountain ranges, from the tropics to the great central plateau Mexico. Guerillas and lancers infested the entire length, and only heavily guarded trains could get through. The surrender of Mexico City did not end the affliction, for Santa Anna took his army to the countryside to join with the guerillas and continue the war.[34]

Although technically no longer a Texas Ranger and now commanding Regulars, Walker continued to use Ranger tactics and his experience in Central Mexico underscores the difficulties faced by General Winfield Scott in maintaining his lines of supply from the coast to Mexico City.

Walker's men encountered a force of some 2,000 Mexican lancers just outside the town of Huamantla. On his own initiative, Walker immediately charged the enemy and forced them to withdraw through the town. Concluding the battle won, Walker unfortunately halted his command in the town to capture some abandoned artillery pieces. The Mexicans unexpectedly counterattacked resulting in Walker's death.[35] Walker's company continued to serve after his death and helped to secure Scott's extended lines of communications from Mexico City to the coast. As it had in Northern Mexico, the United States Army looked to the Texas Rangers to deal with the guerilla problem.

Colonel John C. Hays organized another regiment in July of 1847, and prepared to follow Major Michael Chevallie's Battalion to support General Zachary Taylor's counter-guerilla war in the north. However, in mid August President Polk directed that Hays' regiment be diverted to support Scott in Central Mexico. The War Department ordered Hays to proceed to Vera Cruz "with such of his command as can be spared for the purpose of dispersing the guerillas which infest the line between that place and the interior of Mexico."[36] After an extended overland movement and several delays, Hays landed at Vera Cruz on 17 October and rejoined his regiment, many of whom had arrived a few days prior.[37]

Hays' regiment only comprised five companies, but had a total strength of 580 men.[38] However, few of these men were veterans of frontier service or the earlier battle of Monterey. Some of their deficiency in experience was soon offset by a boost in weapon technology when the military depot at Vera Cruz began issuing Hays' men new Colt revolvers.[39] These weapons, the famed "Walker Colts" of the improved design recommended by their namesake, were soon put to use against Mexican guerillas and bandits. First, Hays spent several days training his men and honing their skills: conducting target practice with the new pistols, operating as a unit, and conducting local patrols. The Ranger patrols soon had the effect of greatly reducing guerilla activity near Vera Cruz, the Mexican irregulars and bandits soon moved on to easier hunting grounds.

Hays' regiment departed Vera Cruz on November 2 at the head of Major General Robert Patterson's volunteer division. The effort to reopen Scott's supply line had begun. The volunteers would garrison the towns along the route to provide rapid reaction forces for convoys under attack and safe havens along the passage, while the Rangers were to scour the countryside and rid it of guerillas. The combined force reached Jalapa on 4 November, and as the Volunteers garrisoned the city the Rangers established their camp. Meanwhile, Hays took two companies and pressed on to Puebla, arriving a few days later.[40]

Hays met with Brigadier General Joseph P. Lane and at Lane's request both men began planning a raid to free some Americans held captive in nearby Izúcar de Matamoros.[42] On 23 November, a combined force of Hays' Rangers and some Louisiana dragoons, accompanied by General Lane, liberated the fifteen American prisoners, captured some artillery, small arms and ammunition, and "killed a good many Mexicans."[43] On their way back to Puebla, two hundred lancers attacked the command. Hays moved to the fore, assumed command, and ordered a charge that drove away the Mexican unit. The charging Rangers chased the Mexicans over a rise where they encountered the main body of the Mexican force; some five hundred lancers. General Lane described the fight in his report,

> When we found it necessary to retire for the purpose of reloading, his men having no sabres [sic], he halted in their rear, and, as the enemy advanced, deliberately shot two of

them dead, and covered his retreat until the arrival of reinforcements.[44]

Hays' cool leadership had again saved the day, the artillery was quickly brought to bear and the Mexicans withdrew. The command returned to Puebla with two killed and two wounded.[45] This mixed force of less than two hundred men had met and defeated five hundred lancers under the command of General J. Rea, and scattered the remaining twelve hundred members of the enemy command, at a cost of only four casualties.[46]

Before moving on to Mexico City, the Rangers undertook a second mission under General Lane. On 21 January, another mixed group of Hays' Rangers and Lane's men, some 350 in all, set out towards Tehuacan in an effort to capture Santa Anna and a force of one hundred cavalry and numerous guerillas. The Rangers rode all night and surrounded the house that they suspected was occupied by Santa Anna, but to no avail. A coach with armed escort that they had earlier stopped, and been ordered to allow to pass because the occupant carried a safe conduct pass issued Brigadier General P. F. Smith, had sent riders ahead to warn Santa Anna.[47] The Mexican General had again eluded capture, but he undoubtedly felt the uncomfortable presence of the Texas Rangers as he made his escape. The Rangers and Volunteers continued on extended patrol through enemy territory for some two weeks before returning to Puebla on February 3rd.[48]

Hays' Rangers resumed their escort duties and arrived in Mexico City on 6 December 1847 at the head of a column of long overdue replacements for Scott's army. Hays' Adjutant, John S. Ford, wrote that the Rangers' entrance into the city "produced a sensation among the inhabitants."[49] The actions of some Rangers soon produced a fair amount of bloodshed as well.

In the city, the Rangers' attitudes and racism caused even more problems than in the field. Adjutant Ford relates three stories: a Ranger accidentally dropped his pistol onto the cobblestone street where it discharged and wounded a Mexican passerby. When a Ranger on horseback took a few candies from the basket a passing Mexican carried on his head, the man became angry that the Ranger was stealing and threw a stone at him, whereupon the Ranger shot and killed him causing a great stampede in the marketplace. And finally, Ford writes that,

> During the evening some rangers were about to enter a theatre. A Mexican sneak thief stole one of their handkerchiefs. The theft was detected. The thief was ordered to stop in Spanish; he ran faster. A six shooter was leveled upon him and discharged. The Mexican dropped lifeless to the pavement. The ranger recovered his handkerchief and went his way as if nothing had happened.[50]

Robert Utley, in analyzing the Rangers' time in Mexico City explains that

> Rangers did not calibrate offenses. The butchery of one of their own in a back alley, an insult, or the theft of a handkerchief all earned the same response, a slug from a heavy Walker Colt. The city's residents did not take kindly to the American occupation, and soldiers who let their guard down could be suddenly stoned from above or shoved into the gutter. As Adjutant John S. Ford recorded, "some gringo lost his life every night."[51]

The harsh treatment of the locals and callous disregard for Mexican lives by some Rangers soon spurred even greater problems and it is quite likely that rather than a deterrent, the Rangers' one slug fits all crimes mentality probably triggered an increase in attacks on Americans.

In the first incident referred to by Utley a Ranger was brutally killed one afternoon in a dangerous back alley area of Mexico City known as "Cutthroat." The Rangers' response was swift and typically violent. The next night a group of fifteen or twenty Texas Rangers entered Cutthroat and began avenging their murdered comrade. A military patrol, upon hearing the firing, confronted the Rangers but instead of putting a halt to the killings joined in. Ford writes that, "In the evening the captain reported more than eighty bodies lying in the morgue. These were parties who had no relatives or friends to care for them."[52] Ford's last sentence implies that the total number killed might have been much higher.

Winfield Scott treated the issue of army discipline in a very different manner than had Zachary Taylor. Shortly after his conquest of Vera Cruz, Scott issued General Order Number 20 proclaiming martial law. Many other orders followed but these were not idle pronouncements. Scott meant to enforce strict rules of behavior on his army and the conquered populace; in April 1847, he had an American soldier hanged for rape.[53] Scott later confronted Hays over the issue of the Rangers' killing of Mexicans in the city, but not about Cutthroat. Hays responded to the accusations by claiming his men acted in self defense and Scott apparently let the matter drop. Scott, apparently discerning Zachary Taylor's most successful technique for dealing with the unruly Rangers, soon realized that busy Rangers employed outside the city caused many fewer problems.

Hays and about sixty five Rangers departed Mexico City in early January 1848 to hunt the elusive Padre Jarauta, a notorious guerilla leader.[54] The Rangers, led by a Mexican guide, marched first to Otumba, in the mountains some sixty miles from Mexico City, and then back to Teotihuacán. The Rangers found the village nearly empty upon their arrival and occupied a large building on the plaza. Weary from their long march the command went to sleep with an inadequate guard. Padre Jarauta and his men seized the opportunity and attacked the Rangers. However, the Rangers reacted quickly and soon turned the tables on their attackers, wounding Jarauta and killing fifteen or twenty of the enemy while suffering no friendly casualties.[55]

The Texas Rangers commenced their last counter-guerilla operation on 17 February 1848. This date is significant because although the Treaty of Guadalupe Hidalgo (which ended the Mexican war) was signed on 2 February 1848, the treaty was not yet ratified by Mexico or the United States and so the Rangers continued to fight.[56] The last Ranger operation of the war had as its objective the destruction of Padre Jarauta's band of guerillas. The Padre, having recovered from his wounds and seemingly determined to carry on the fight despite the impending peace was reported to be located at Zacualtipán with 450 men so Hays and Lane again joined forces to destroy the guerilla chieftain. A force of 250 rangers and 130 Dragoons assaulted Zacualtipán just after daylight on 25 February. A bitter house to house battle ensued in which Jarauta again narrowly escaped. However, his command was effectively destroyed; General Lane reported 150 Mexicans killed, 50 taken prisoner, and many more wounded. Lane's and Hays' commands suffered a combined total of five wounded, one mortally.[57] The Texas Rangers' last battle of the Mexican War had been a remarkable victory.

The Texas Rangers, during this final phase of the Mexican War, again contributed to the success and security of the conventional force by undertaking difficult counter-guerilla operations, operations for which they were uniquely suited. However, the Rangers also proved again that an unconventional force such as theirs was also wholly unsuited for occupation duty in enemy cities. Individual Rangers committed several unnecessary killings while in Mexico City and a group of Rangers led a reprisal against the inhabitants of Cutthroat, but none of these actions were authorized by the Rangers' leaders even if the reprisal may have been condoned by Texan and American authorities after the fact. It is interesting to note that President Polk himself directed that the Texas Rangers be sent to Central Mexico to deal with the guerilla problem even though he surely read all of Taylor's reports from northern Mexico bemoaning the Rangers' problems there. President Polk and General Scott were therefore apparently comfortable that regardless of the methods employed by the Rangers their ultimate success in eliminating or suppressing the guerilla problem justified any excesses.

Leadership mattered in this phase of the war as it had in all previous phases. Although Hays and Ford did not prevent the reprisal against Cutthroat, they did not lead it. Moreover, unlike "Mustang" Gray's indiscriminate murder of the nearest Mexicans at hand, the Rangers in Mexico City targeted those most directly responsible for the murder of their comrade and thus elicited very little outcry over their actions. Most telling of all, however, is the impact of Ranger leadership at the very close of the war. On 25 April 1848, Santa Anna made his way along the National Road as he traveled into exile yet again for disappointing his countrymen. A large group of Texas Rangers under the command of Adjutant Ford traveled the same road. The men decided to kill Santa Anna in revenge for the Alamo, the Goliad Massacre, and all of the other pain and death wrought by Santa Anna in Mexico's struggles against Texas.

Ford knew he had to act swiftly or be a party to an unlawful murder after the termination of the war. He rode to the head of the assembled Rangers and said,

> Yes, that is admitted [the crimes of Santa Anna mentioned above], but did not the world condemn General Santa Anna for this cruel butchery of prisoners? That was a stain upon his reputation as a soldier. Now, was it not considered an act of magnanimity on the part of the government of the Republic of Texas when its officials liberated General Santa Anna after what happened? Reflect a moment. General Santa Anna dishonored himself by murdering prisoners of war; will you not dishonor Texas and ourselves by killing him? . . . You would dishonor Texas.[58]

The Texans lined both sides of the road and as the carriage carrying the disgraced former ruler of Mexico went by the Rangers stood in eerie silence, never uttering a single word. Santa Anna was allowed to pass unharmed through the ranks of his former foes and into exile.

CHAPTER 8 - ANALYSIS AND CONCLUSIONS

The Texas Rangers were undeniably effective in combat during the Mexican War. They acquired and reported intelligence on enemy activities, strength, location and probable intentions that no other unit of the American forces could have supplied. They helped to suppress enemy intelligence operations by operating against enemy regular and irregular units from the opening days of the war to the very last. They also served to expedite the passage of conventional forces through enemy territory by reconnoitering routes, screening against enemy units, and occasionally even guarding the main body of conventional troops against enemy cavalry attack. In the dismounted role, they were the equal of the Regulars in assaulting Federation and Independence Hills outside Monterey, and they surpassed those same Regulars when the fighting moved into the streets of the city. Looking back to Dr. Huber's description of the contributions of irregular forces in Compound Warfare, "In sum, the guerilla force enhances the effort of the main force by offering information . . . and troops, and denying them to the enemy," Texas Rangers conferred all of these advantages on the armies of Zachary Taylor and Winfield Scott.[1]

Overall, the Rangers greatly facilitated American success on the field of battle, but the question of whether the actions of certain small groups of Rangers impeded the overall war effort is more difficult to evaluate. The Rangers fought as an unconventional force during most of their Mexican War experience, and as such they experienced many of the problems inherent in unconventional war. The Texas Rangers did not impede American commanders in winning the war. In fact, Benjamin McCulloch's crucial reconnaissance to locate and appraise Santa Anna's army before the battle of Buena Vista helped to prevent a major American defeat. However, it is probable that the actions of individuals, small groups, and, in the case of Mabry B. Gray's unit, a company did impede the winning of the "peace." The harsh, callous treatment and occasional outright murder of Mexican civilians by some Texas Rangers, and the widespread perception that such actions were condoned by both the Rangers' leadership and their American commanders likely did much to stiffen Mexican resistance during the war. Reprisals, thefts, and murders probably contributed to increases in the strength of guerilla units and other more subtle forms of resistance, although the degree to which such actions might have caused the foregoing problems is difficult or impossible to determine. That the actions of these men left a black mark on the reputation of the Rangers and the American conduct of the war is indisputable.

It is also undeniable that many of the men who comprised the various units of Texas Rangers that fought in the Mexican War lacked discipline. The majority of the problems attributed to the Rangers occurred not in the field or in combat but in the towns while the men were off duty. This then was a problem of individual discipline, not unit discipline. This distinction is not meant to exonerate the unit commanders of their responsibility for the actions of their men (on or off duty) but rather to highlight the difference between actions by the men and actions by the organization. Atrocities perpetrated with the knowledge and leadership of the unit's commanders are very different indeed than atrocities committed by individuals or small groups without the approval of their leaders. In evaluating the unit discipline of the Texas Rangers, a very different conclusion emerges. In combat, the Rangers showed a degree of discipline under fire that few other units of the American army could equal. Assaulting fortified enemy positions under direct fire, charging a numerically superior enemy, leading the attack in street by street fighting in a fortified town, and conducting extended patrols deep in enemy territory far from reinforcements and in small numbers are all examples of very high levels of unit discipline. In fact, each of the examples above illustrates exactly why the Rangers were so valuable to their American commanders.

With the exception of the Marin massacre perpetrated by Mabry B. Gray's unit, all other atrocities or acts of ill discipline charged against the Rangers concerned individual or small groups and did not involve the Rangers' leadership. However, it is important to note that, both as individuals and as units, the Texas Rangers (and other volunteers from Texas) operated under a very different concept of acceptable behavior in wartime than their American counterparts, Regular or Volunteer. The United States Army's concept of the conduct of warfare derived from its European roots and influences: uniformed forces assembling for battle, the role of honor between combatants, the protection of innocents, prisoners, and wounded. The Rangers concept of warfare differed completely in every aspect. The Texas Rangers and their foes, Mexican irregulars and bandits, wore no uniforms and therefore the enemy was distinguishable from the civilian populace only by their actions or after identification by someone (friend or foe) willing to denounce them as a raider, thief, or guerilla. The Rangers, long taught by their foes to expect no honor on the battlefield, might have been expected to exhibit none. Although, to a remarkable degree, they did exhibit such honor. The Comanches never surrendered, and invariably killed and mutilated any enemy wounded left on the field. The Mexicans had a long history of killing Texan wounded and prisoners (even killing American wounded during the battle of Monterey), and they used surrender as a ruse to escape destruction of their forces.[2] Yet the Rangers did not refuse to take prisoners or kill those prisoners they took. Instead, they disdained taking prisoners in large numbers because as a mounted force, usually operating beyond friendly lines, they had no capacity to feed or transport prisoners. The Texas Rangers did take prisoners on select occasions: to interrogate them for information or to prevent them for compromising the security of an operation. Such prisoners were either later set free or turned over to Taylor's army. Although there is innuendo, there are no confirmed accounts or even accusations of the Texas Rangers killing prisoners or wounded during the Mexican War.

Another possible explanation for the crimes committed by some Rangers (and other volunteers) is simple racism. The men of the Mexican War (on all sides) lived and fought under very different concepts of race than now exist at the beginning of the 21st Century. Racism was a prevalent and accepted social viewpoint in the mid-1800s. In fact, the American concept of Manifest Destiny promulgated racial arguments to legitimize not one but two wars of conquest against "inferior" races. The American Indian and the Mexican were both judged to be "lesser civilizations" (largely due to their race) and to be deficient in the use of their land. Thus, Americans had the right, and even the obligation, to impose a superior culture (and race). It is therefore unsurprising that many men entered Mexican War service with strong racial prejudices. This is not meant to judge, it is unfair and pointless to evaluate these men and their actions based on modern concepts of culture and race; they simply did not share these views.

Yet a second aspect of racism is more troubling; the denigration of the enemy. This is not new to American military history, as James McCaffery notes,

> American soldiery during the Mexican War was not very different from the volunteer soldiers throughout American history. They believed themselves invincible in battle, and they complained about the food, their superiors, the weather, and the character of the enemy they faced. They viewed the enemy as being on a lower plane, and they therefore found it easier to hate and kill in far off Mexico.[3]

McCaffery goes on to add another dimension to the psychology of combat during the Mexican War. He notes that those who did not take part in major battles were more likely to vent their frustrations and passions on civilians. This might have affected the men of the later Ranger companies who fought Taylor's counter-guerilla war since they missed the battles of Monterey and Buena Vista. The later volunteers from Texas may have operated under a second strain, the need to avenge the death of a relative or loved one, and denied the legitimate use of force in battle they may have murdered Mexican civilians to assuage their anger.[4] This is not meant to condone these crimes, merely to offer some rationale for why they occurred.

American commanders, faced with incorporating a very unconventional force into their very conventional armies, integrated the Texas Rangers in markedly different ways. Each commander utilized the unique skills and attributes of the Rangers to the best of their ability based on their different circumstances and predilections. Zachary Taylor allowed the Rangers to operate independently as irregular cavalry during much of his northern campaign. When he chose to incorporate the Rangers into his battle plans (Monterey and Buena Vista) he maintained unit integrity. The Rangers performed admirably in both battles and escaped censure or accusation of impropriety. However, when operating independently they caused Taylor grief.

Although Taylor disdained the methods employed by the Rangers, he was content to use the Rangers to get his dirty work done, even retaining the services of the notorious "Mustang" Gray. What he failed to do was to recognize the radically different concept of counter-guerilla warfare under which the Rangers operated. In turn, he failed to set and enforce clear guidelines for the conduct of the counter-guerilla war or issue "rules of engagement" type orders. Taylor, having also failed to assign observers or attach American units to Ranger missions, instead found himself trying to evaluate charges of crimes based on testimony of enemy civilian authorities or the Ranger participants. Having created an untenable situation, Taylor fell into the habit of chastising entire units and publicly lamenting atrocities, rather than holding individuals accountable, or taking actions to identify and punish the guilty parties and/or prevent future incidents. Taylor's method of handling the Texas Rangers boiled down to creating plausible deniability for himself, and it worked.

Taylor shrewdly fought a bloody counter-guerilla war while protecting his own reputation. Here the Rangers again performed valuable service, this time as the scapegoat. Unfortunately for the early Rangers, their hard won battlefield reputation as brave and dependable soldiers was unfairly tarnished by the actions of later units and a commander who used them to deflect criticism of his conduct of the counter-guerilla war.

Winfield Scott's experience with the Texas Rangers was much shorter, and differed in many ways. The Texas Rangers joined Scott's army only some four months before the end of the war, but still found time to cause him trouble. Scott, the most experienced general in the United States Army, developed a plan to use General Joseph Lane as his de facto "chief of counter-guerilla operations," and the Rangers conducted most of their missions in Scott's theater as part of Lane's command.[5] In contrast to Taylor, Lane chose to conduct combined, task force type operations in which mixed units of Rangers, Volunteer Cavalry, and occasionally Infantry all took part. Moreover, Lane commanded many of the operations in person. This allowed Lane to enforce his own concept of the rules of war (presumably one shared and endorsed by Scott) and not just accept those of the Rangers after the fact. Although the results of just one such question of the rules of war led to Padre Jarauta's escape (allowing the carriage with a safe conduct letter to pass, which later alerted the guerilla leader), Lane's presence and influence likely prevented other questionable actions by the Rangers. Additionally, Lane's presence almost certainly dispelled many false accusations of misconduct on the part of disgruntled Mexican villagers, few questions or difficult decisions here; Lane knew first hand what had happened. The addition of conventional forces, although acting in an unconventional role, probably did impede the effectiveness and mobility of the Texas Rangers to a slight degree, but it also shielded them from the kinds of criticisms suffered during Taylor's campaign. While it is highly unlikely that Taylor would have joined the Rangers on their operations, he might have assigned a ranking subordinate such a job, as Scott later did, and saved himself many problems.

Finally, it is clear that strong decisive leadership served to reduce problems, even though it did not prevent some incidents from occurring. The various Ranger organizations serving under Zachary Taylor may have lacked such leadership at the higher level (as it applied to them) but men like John Hays, Samuel Walker, and Ben McCulloch provided very strong leadership at the organizational level and fewer problems occurred during their tenures. As Captain Walter Lane and Mabry Gray arrived the same lack of leadership at the top existed but at this point the Rangers also lacked strong leadership at the organizational level and the result was a greater number of problems. Turning to Scott's theater, the Rangers enjoyed strong leadership at the higher level (Generals Scott and Lane) and at the organizational level (Hays and Walker) and the Rangers garnered fewer charges of atrocities during this phase. To come to the point, the fewest problems occurred in an atmosphere of strong higher level (Army and Division) leadership combined with strong organizational leadership while the most problems occurred in an atmosphere of weak leadership at these same levels. However, leadership was not the only causal factor and the nature of the conflict varied greatly between phases and by theaters but leadership did matter; strong leaders developed more disciplined units whereas a lack of leadership at crucial levels left other units more vulnerable to problems.

In summary, the Texas Rangers were very effective in combat, but the tactics, techniques, and procedures that made them effective also likely fueled Mexican resistance to a certain degree making the peace harder to win. Some of the harsh nature of the Rangers' combat behavior is attributable to the "culture" of the time and some attributable to the Rangers' unique historical experience. However, many, if not all of the Rangers' tactics, techniques, and procedures had been developed and refined during their many years of what amounted to counter-guerilla warfare in Texas and thus may simply have reflected the nature of this type of unconventional warfare as practiced at that time.

The modern day relevance of an analysis of the Texas Rangers' combat record during the Mexican War may seem remote, but the opposite is true. As the United States Army completes its combat operations in Iraq in the Spring of 2003, it seems increasingly likely that future phases of the Global War on Terrorism will be less conventional in nature. Such wars will almost certainly employ forms of Compound Warfare as the American military seeks to destroy terrorist enclaves and safe havens in distant lands. American commanders will increasingly be called upon to conduct combat operations with allies and coalition partners who do not share our concepts of the rules of warfare. Additionally, many of the military organizations with whom we will operate will bring their own unique set of skills and attributes to the fight along with their prejudices and weaknesses. We will seldom have the luxury of choosing our allies. Instead we must learn to capitalize on the strengths and compensate for their shortcomings while striving to prevent violations of the rules of war. This analysis of the Mexican War and the role of the Texas Rangers offers many hard won lessons for the commanders of today regarding the integration, control and utilization of coalition and irregular forces.

More than two thousand years ago Sun Tzu wrote, "Know the enemy and know yourself; in a hundred battles you will never be in peril."[6] To this I would add, "Know your allies." Without an understanding of the capabilities, limitations and prejudices of coalition or allied partners, problems and charges of atrocities like those that plagued Zachary Taylor are likely to arise, and Taylor's coalition partners (the Texas Rangers) even shared the same language, culture, and religious background!

Every situation will differ in important ways, but several generalities are clear. First, establish, disseminate, and enforce clear standards of conduct on and off the field of battle. Winfield Scott imposed martial law in conquered areas (applying to military and civilians alike) and enforced the laws he established, even though both he and Taylor lacked the explicit legal authority to do so. Zachary Taylor established few standards and enforced fewer still, preferring to banish troublesome units to distant regions and discharge the worst individual offenders who then made their way back to the border (or wherever they went) completely free of whatever limited control they had previously been under. Although Scott's system was not perfect, it is little wonder that it produced better results.

Second, determine what the problems are and apply corrective measures. This seems simplistic but it worked for both Taylor and Scott. If the Rangers caused trouble in the towns when they are off duty, commanders should have gotten them out of the towns and kept them on duty, in the field and on the trail of the enemy. Scott seems to have learned this lesson more rapidly than Taylor (although Scott ostensibly did have the benefit of Taylor's experience), but both men used this technique to good advantage. It is interesting to note that, with the possible exception of Captain Lane's complaint about being sent on a risky deep reconnaissance mission, the Rangers did not complain; this is what they joined these armies to do.

Third, hold units and leaders accountable. Hays, Walker, McCulloch, Chevallie and Captain Lane all expected to be held accountable for the actions of their men and they accepted that responsibility; after all, these men were the commanders. This sense of responsibility gave Taylor and Scott a means of controlling the actions of these units and applying corrective measures as necessary. When Zachary Taylor failed to hold Mustang Gray accountable for the actions of his men, whom he likely led during the massacre, Taylor not only failed in his responsibilities, but set a dangerous precedent for other units. Appeals to the honor of the coalition partners, their organizations, or to their religious obligations might also be effective. Adjutant Ford's appeal to uphold the honor of Texas probably saved Santa Anna's life. By the same token, if they dishonor or detract from the overall war effort, those units should be disbanded or discharged from service, and their commanders should be tried in the appropriate courts.

Fourth, know your allies' prejudices. Had American commanders fully realized the bitter nature of the War for Texas Independence and the decade of intervening conflict along the border, they might have realized the likelihood of reprisals and atrocities against civilians, or at least acknowledged what signs to look for. Had they been armed with this knowledge, both Taylor and Scott would have been much better prepared to prevent such actions rather than deal with them only after they had occurred.

The Texas Rangers cut a large path through the history of the Mexican War and created an enduring reputation, some of it deserved, some of it not. Their combat record is top notch; tough, courageous fighters with the leadership, discipline and firepower to win where others could not. Their reputation for ill discipline and excess is for the most part overblown, although several very serious incidents did occur. Perhaps the greatest evaluation of their wartime service came from those with and for whom they served. General Taylor, General Scott, Secretary of War Marcy, and President Polk all weighed the advantages and disadvantages to be gained by employing the Texas Rangers in combat in the Mexican War and all four men came to the same conclusion; the benefits of the Rangers' service outweighed the costs. For them, the Texas Rangers were no mixed blessing at all.[7]

FOOTNOTES

Chapter 1 Footnotes

1. Jack K. Bauer, *The Mexican War, 1846-1848,* 10.
2. Carol and Thomas Christensen, *The U.S.-Mexican War*, 2.
3. Based on the author's personal experience as a Latin American Foreign Area Officer and interviews conducted with Embassy Officers in Mexico City in March, 2002.
4. Frederick Wilkins, *Highly Irregular Regulars: the Texas Rangers in the Mexican War,* 2.
5. Thomas W. Cutrer, *Ben McCulloch and the Frontier Military Tradition*, 61-62.
6. Cutrer, 62.
7. Walter Prescott Webb, *The Texas Rangers in the Mexican War*, 8.
8. Wilkins, 29.
9. Charles D. Spurlin, *Texas Volunteers in the Mexican War,* 19, 104.
10. Cutrer, 88, 92.
11. Thomas M. Huber, *Compound Warfare Anthology*, introduction. https://cgsc2.leavenworth.army.mil/csi/research/ComWar/comwarintrohuber.asp
12. James M. McCaffery, *Army of Manifest Destiny*, 125.

Chapter 2 Footnotes

1. William Henry, *The Texas Rangers,* 9.
2. Christensen, *The U.S.-Mexican War*, 15.

3. For a list of casualty numbers for the battles cited see The Handbook of Texas Online, available at http://www.tsha.utexas.edu/handbook/online/
4. Christensen, *The U.S.-Mexican War*, 42.
5. Cutrer, 47.
6. Henry, 10.
7. Charles Weber, "My First Day with the Rangers," American Review, Vol. I, No. 3, March 1845.
8. Joseph E. Bennett, "The Best of the Early Rangers," 20.
9. Robert M. Utley, *Lone Star Justice*, 59.
10. James K. Greer, *Texas Ranger: Jack Hays in the Frontier Southwest*, 126-128. Utley, 60.
11. Samuel C. Reid, *Scouting Expeditions of McCulloch's Texas Rangers*, 38.
12. Henry, *The Texas Rangers*, 85-86, 88.
13. Wilkins, 41-42.
14. Charles D. Spurlin, *Texas Volunteers in the Mexican War*, 150-161.
15. Utley, 63-65.

Chapter 3 Footnotes

1. Huber, introduction, 1.
2. Cutrer, 67.
3. Wilkins, 191.
4. Huber, introduction, 2.

Chapter 4 Footnotes

1. Utley, 64.
2. Ronnie C. Tyler, et al, *The New Handbook of Texas; vol. 6*, 797.
3. Tyler, et al, 797; Utley, 59.
4. Webb, 6-7; Charles E. Heller and William A. Stofft, eds, *America's First Battles, 1776-1965*, 64-65.
5. Bauer, 48.

6. Zachary Taylor, Official Report of the Battle of Palo Alto, May 16, 1846, 1.
7. John Edwards Weems, *To Conquer a Peace: The War Between the United States and Mexico,* 133-134, 136.
8. Zachary Taylor, Official Report of the Battle of Resaca de la Palma, May 17, 1846, 3.
9. Webb, 14.
10. Webb, 18.
11. Map, "Mexican War," United States Combat Institute Studies.
12. Webb, 24.
13. Webb, 27.
14. Webb, 28.
15. McCulloch, letter from Camargo dated 27 July 1846.
16. Cutrer, 75.
17. Cutrer, 75.
18. Webb, 29.
19. Greer, 130.
20. Caruso, 88. Utley, 63, Tyler, et al, *The New Handbook of Texas; vol. 4,* 385.
21. Webb, 31.

Chapter 5 Footnotes

1. Wilkins, 81.
2. Maurice Matlof, ed, *American Military History,* 168.
3. Greer, 141; Cutrer, 83; Wilkins, 89; Robert M. Utley states that "Seven took lance wounds, but not one lost his life." Utley 69.
4. John S. D. Eisenhower, *So Far From God: The U.S. War with Mexico 1846- 1848,* 131.
5. Utley, 69.
6. Webb, 45, 55; Spurlin, 95-96; Greer, 148; Lavender, 110.
7. Greer, 141.

8. Greer, 136; David Lavender, *Climax at Buena Vista; the American Campaigns in Northeastern Mexico 1846-47*, 103, 108.
9. Map, "Battle of Monterrey," *Personal Memoirs of Ulysses S. Grant.*
10. Utley, 69; Lavender, 110; Luther Giddings, *Sketches of the campaign in northern Mexico*, 192; Webb, 46.
11. Greer, 143; Webb, 46; Lavender, 110; Cutrer, 83; Christensen, 132.
12. Spurlin, 82.
13. Wilkins, 91.
14. Webb, 47.
15. Spurlin, 86; Greer, 144; Eisenhower, 130.
16. Webb, 49.
17. Spurlin, 86.
18. Spurlin, 90.
19. Greer, 147; Hays learned this trick from the Comanches, he eluded a similar trap in 1840 at the Battle of Walker Creek. Ten Comanche warriors attempted to lure Hays' fourteen men into an ambush but he held them back. Some seventy Indians next charged Hays' Rangers from their concealed positions. Hays' men wheeled and attacked the Indians in the flanks killing several with their Colt revolvers and forcing a brief respite in the fight. Hays' men were now low on ammunition but the Indian's leader continued to press his warriors to attack. Hays ordered "any man who has a load, kill that chief." Robert Ad Gillespie responded "I'll do it" and despite a painful lance wound took steady aim and killed the Comanche chief with one shot. Their leader killed, the attack was broken and the remaining Comanche warriors withdrew. Utley, 10-12.
20. Utley, 71-72; Webb, 53-54.
21. Eisenhower, 135.

22. Giddings, 160, 162.
23. Lavender, 112-113.
24. Eisenhower, 138; Lavender, 114.
25. Eisenhower, 140.
26. Greer, 143-4.
27. Cutrer, 86.
28. Wilkins, 98.
29. Webb, 55.
30. Greer, 148.
31. Greer, 150.
32. Greer, 150.
33. Webb, 57.
34. Greer, 152.
35. Eisenhower, 146-7.
36. Greer, 152.
37. Lavender, 120.
38. Eisenhower, 147.
39. Utley, 73; Cutrer, 87.
40. Giddings, 212.
41. Cutrer, 87.
42. Greer, 152.
43. Utley, 73.
44. Greer, 154.
45. Bauer, 101.
46. Cutrer, 88.
47. Lavender, 280-281.
48. Bauer, 102.
49. Utley, 75-6.

Chapter 6 Footnotes

1. Lavender, 125.
2. Lavender, 127, 129.
3. Lavender, 134.
4. Wilkins, 123.
5. Wilkins, 123.
6. Webb, 62.

7. Webb, 63; Lavender, 130-1.
8. Bauer, 206.
9. Lavender, 166.
10. Bauer, 206.
11. Cutrer, 91.
12. Utley, 76.
13. Taylor, Buena Vista, 5.
14. Cutrer, 92.
15. Utley, 76.
16. Webb, 63.
17. Webb, 66 cites sixteen men, Cutrer on page 94 cites fourteen.
18. Webb, 64.
19. Cutrer, 95.
20. Webb, 66; Cutrer, 94; Lavender, 169.
21. Webb, 66.
22. Utley, 76; Cutrer, 95.
23. Map, "The Mexican War, Taylor's Campaign March 1846 – February 1847," available at http://www.dean.usma.edu/history/dhistorymaps/MexicanW/mexw2l.htm
24. Cutrer, 96; Spurlin, 254.
25. Cutrer, 96.
26. Cutrer, 96.
27. Cutrer, 96; Webb, 67-8.
28. Cutrer, 98.
29. Cutrer, 96.
30. Cutrer, 98.
31. Webb, 68.
32. Cutrer, 99, 100.
33. The American light artillery batteries of six pound guns were known as "flying" batteries for their rapid mobility due to the fact that the entire crew was mounted on horses as opposed to riding on the caissons.
34. Taylor, Buena Vista, 1.

35. Cutrer, 103.
36. Webb, 67.
37. Cutrer, 103.
38. Webb, 14.

Chapter 7 Footnotes

1. Utley (77) lists the date of the massacre as 22 February 1847. Chance (172) lists the date as 24 February even though Samuel Curtis (upon whose diary Chance's account is written) list the date as the 23rd (Chance, 156.). I choose to use the date cited by Curtis. Wilkins, 136.
2. Bauer (218) states "forty or fifty," Utley (77) states 100, but Giddings (291) states fifty so again I choose to cite the participant's account.
3. Chance, 156.
4. Chance, 174-175.
5. Chance, 113.
6. Spurlin, 226-237.
7. Wilkins, 138; Spurlin, 272.
8. Giddings, 324.
9. Giddings, 325-325.
10. Utley, 77; Giddings, 325; Chance, 173.
11. Utley, 78.
12. Utley, 78.
13. Lane, 46-46.
14. Lane, 46.
15. The Mexicans stated that they were "well to do ranchers and were tired of Flores' depredations upon them" Lane, 46.
16. Lane, 48.
17. Lane, 49.
18. Lane, 49.
19. Lane, 49.
20. Lane, 50.
21. Lane, 51.

22. Lane, 52.
23. Lane, 55.
24. Spurlin, 121.
25. Utley, 78.
26. Bauer, 208.
27. Bauer, 204.
28. Bauer, 221; McCaffery, 125; Christensen, 76, 145-146; Lavender, 90.
29. Thomas Cutrer cites Taylor's letter of June 1847 when discussing the Rangers' actions at Matamoros and Reynosa, thus confusing what Taylor said about later Rangers with problems regarding earlier groups. Cutrer, 73-74.
30. Chance, 174.
31. Matloff, et al, 174.
32. Matloff, et al, 174-178.
33. Webb, 74.
34. Utley, 79.
35. Bauer, *The Mexican War, 1846-1848*. 329-331.
36. Greer, 169.
37. Greer, 170.
38. John S. Ford, *Rip Ford's Texas*, 73.
39. Greer, 170.
40. Greer, 174.
41. Map, "Scott's Campaign", West Point Military Academy, History Dept.
42. Greer, 175-176
43. Ford, 78.
44. Webb, 83.
45. Webb, 83.
46. Greer, 178.
47. Webb, 83.
48. Webb, 84.
49. Ford, 81.
50. Ford, 81-82.
51. Utley, 81-83.

52. Spurlin, 131; Ford, 84.
53. Eisenhower, 266.
54. Utley, 83.
55. Ford, 89.
56. Ford, 91; Utley, 83.
57. Utley, 84.
58. Ford, 103.

Chapter 8 Footnotes

1. Huber, 2.
2. Giddings, 181.
3. McCaffery, 210.
4. McCaffery, 127-128.
5. Utley, 80.
6. Samuel B. Griffin, *Sun Tzu, The Art of War*, Oxford University Press: London, 1963, 84.
7. This paper was editing for spelling and grammar with Microsoft Word 2000 spell check feature. This paper was proofread by Ward D. Ferguson.

Bibliography
Primary Sources

Chance, Joseph E., ed. *Mexico Under Fire: being the diary of Samuel Ryan Curtis, 3rd Ohio Volunteer Regiment, during the American military occupation of northern Mexico, 1846-1847.* Fort Worth, Texas: Texas Christian University Press, 1994.

Ford, John Salmon. *Rip Ford's Texas.* Austin, Texas: University of Texas Press, 1987.

George, Isaac B., *Heroes and Incidents of the Mexican War, containing Doniphan's Expedition.* Hollywood, CA: 1971.

Giddings, Luther. *Sketches of the campaign in northern Mexico: in eighteen hundred forty-six and seven / by an officer of the First Regiment of Ohio volunteers.* New York: Putnam and Co., 1853.

Grant, Ulysses S. *Personal Memoirs of Ulysses S. Grant.* Princeton, NJ: Collectors Reprints, 1998.

Kendall, George Wilkins. *Dispatches from the Mexican War.* Norman, Oklahoma: University of Oklahoma Press, 1999.

Lane, Walter P. *The Adventures and Recollections of General Walter P. Lane, a San Jacinto Veteran.* Marshall, Texas: Tri-Weekly Herald, 1887.

McCulloch, Ben. Ben and Henry Eustace McCulloch Family Papers, 1798-1961. Box 3G37, Center for American History, University of Texas at Austin.

Reid, Samuel Chester. *The Scouting Expeditions of McCulloch's Texas Rangers; or the Summer and Fall Campaigns of the Army of the United States in Mexico.* New York: 1885.

Taylor, Zachary. *Letters of Zachary Taylor, from the battlefields of the Mexican War.* Rochester, New York: The Genesee Press, 1908.

Taylor, Zachary. Official Report of the Battle of Palo Alto, May 16, 1846. Documents of the U.S.-Mexican War, Descendants of Mexican War Veterans website: http://www.dmwv.org/mexwar/documents/docs.htm

Taylor, Zachary. Official Report of the Battle of Resaca de la Palma, May 17, 1846. Documents of the U.S.-Mexican War, Descendants of Mexican War Veterans website: http://www.dmwv.org/mexwar/documents/docs.htm

Taylor, Zachary. Official Report of the Battle for Monterey, September 25, 1846. Documents of the U.S.-Mexican War, Descendants of Mexican War Veterans website: http://www.dmwv.org/mexwar/documents/docs.htm

Taylor, Zachary. Official Report of the Battle of Buena Vista, March 6, 1847. Documents of the U.S.-Mexican War, Descendants of Mexican War Veterans website: http://www.dmwv.org/mexwar/documents/docs.htm

Weber, Charles Wilkins. "My First Day with the Rangers." American Review, Volume I, Number 3, March 1845.

Wilson, James C. "Address on Removing the Remains of Captains Walker and Gillespie, on the 21st of April, A. D. 1856." San Antonio Ledger, 1856.

Secondary Sources

Alcaraz, Ramon. *The Other Side: or, Notes for the History of the War between Mexico and the United States, Written in Mexico.* New York: B. Franklin, 1970.

Barton, Henry W. *Texas Volunteers in the Mexican War.* Wichita Falls, Texas: Texian Press, 1970.

Bauer, K. Jack. *The Mexican War, 1846-1848.* Lincoln, NE: University of Nebraska Press, 1992.

Caruso, A. Brooke. *The Mexican Spy Company: United States Covert Operations in Mexico, 1845-1848.* Jefferson, North Carolina: McFarland & Company, 1991.

Christensen, Carol and Thomas. *The U.S.-Mexican War.* San Francisco: Bay Books, 1998.

Cutrer, Thomas W. *Ben McCulloch and the Frontier Military Tradition.* Chapel Hill, North Carolina: University of North Carolina Press, 1993.

Dana, Edmund L. "Incidents in the Life of Captain Samuel H. Walker, Texan Ranger, killed at the Battle of Huamantla, Mexico." <u>Wyoming Historical and Geological Society Proceedings.</u> Wilkes-Barre, Pennsylvania: Wyoming Historical and Geological Society, 1882.

Dillon, Lester R. *American Artillery in the Mexican War, 1846-1847*. Austin, Texas: Presidial Press, 1975.

Eisenhower, John S. D. *So Far From God: The U.S. War with Mexico 1846-1848*. New York: Random House, 1989.

Greer, James K. *Texas Ranger: Jack Hays in the Frontier Southwest*. College Station, Texas: Texas A&M University Press, 1993.

Hardin, Stephen. *The Texas Rangers*. Oxford, United Kingdom: Osprey Publishing, 1991.

Heller, Charles E. and Stofft, William A., eds. *America's First Battles, 1776-1965*. Lawrence, KS: University Press of Kansas, 1986.

Henry, Will. *The Texas Rangers*. New York: Random House, 1957.

Huber, Thomas M. "Compound Warfare Anthology." United States Army Combat Studies Institute website. https://cgsc2.leavenworth.army.mil/csi/research/Com War/comwarintrohuber.asp

Johannsen, Robert Walter. *To the Halls of Montezuma: The Mexican War in the American Imagination*. New York: Oxford University Press, 1985.

Lavender, David. *Climax at Buena Vista; the American Campaigns in Northeastern Mexico 1846-47*. Philadelphia; J. B. Lippincott Company, 1966.

Matloff, Maurice, ed. *American Military History.* Washington: United States Army Center of Military History, 1988.

McCaffery, James M. *Army of Manifest Destiny: The American Soldier in the Mexican War, 1846-1848.* New York: New York University Press, 1992.

Meed, Douglas V. *The Mexican War 1846-1848.* Oxford, United Kingdom: Osprey Publishing, 2002.

Oates, Stephen B. "The Texas Rangers in the Mexican War." Texas Military History. 1963, Volume 3, Series 2, pages 65-84.

Robinson, Cecil. *The View from Chapultepec: Mexican Writers on the Mexican-American War.* Tucson: University of Arizona Press, 1989.

Rose, Victor M. *The Life and Services of Gen. Ben McCulloch.* Austin, Texas: The Steck Company, 1958.

Spurlin, Charles D. *Texas Volunteers in the Mexican War.* Austin, Texas: Eakin Press, 1998.

Spurlin, Charles D. *Texas Veterans in the Mexican War*: *muster rolls of Texas military units.* Saint Louis, Missouri: Ingmire Publications, 1984.

Tyler, Ronnie C., et al. *The New Handbook of Texas; vols. 4, 6.* Austin, Texas: State Historical Association, 1996.

Utley, Robert M. *Lone Star Justice: the First Century of the Texas Rangers.* New York: Oxford University Press, 2002.

Webb, Walter Prescott. *Texas Rangers: a Century of Frontier Defense.* Austin, Texas: University of Texas Press, 1965.

Webb, Walter Prescott. *The Texas Rangers in the Mexican War.* Austin, Texas: Jenkins Garret Press, 1975.

Weems, John Edwards. *To Conquer a Peace: The War Between the United States and Mexico.* Garden City, N.Y.: Doubleday, 1974.

Wilkins, Frederick *Highly Irregular Regulars: the Texas Rangers in the Mexican War.* Austin, Texas: Eakin Press, 1990.

Winders, Richard Bruce. *Mr. Polk's Army: The American Military Experience in the Mexican War.* College Station, Texas: Texas A&M University Press, 1997.

Made in the USA
Middletown, DE
18 October 2015